DATE DUE

MAY 1 7 2009	
NOV 2 3 2009	
Dec 18, 2014	
FEB 2 8 2017	
MAY 0 4 2017	

RACE AND RACISM
IN LITERATURE

Recent Contributions in
Exploring Social Issues through Literature

Literature and the Environment
George Hart and Scott Slovic, editors

Youth Gangs in Literature
Claudia Durst Johnson

Bioethics and Medical Issues in Literature
Mahala Yates Stripling

RACE AND RACISM IN LITERATURE

Charles E. Wilson, Jr.

Exploring Social Issues through Literature
Claudia Durst Johnson, Series Editor

GREENWOOD PRESS
Westport, Connecticut • London

Library of Congress Cataloging-in-Publication Data

Wilson, Charles E., 1961–
    Race and racism in literature / Charles E. Wilson, Jr.
        p. cm.—(Exploring social issues through literature ; ISSN 1551–0263)
    Includes bibliographical references and index.
    ISBN 0–313–32820–X
    1. American literature—History and criticism. 2. Racism in literature. 3. Literature
and society—United States. 4. Race in literature. I. Title. II. Series.
PS169.R28W55   2005
8109´3552—dc22   2005001494

British Library Cataloguing in Publication Data is available.

Library of Congress Catalog Card Number: 2005001494
ISBN: 0–313–32820–X
ISSN: 1551–0263

First published in 2005

Greenwood Press, 88 Post Road West, Westport, CT 06881
An imprint of Greenwood Publishing Group, Inc.
www.greenwood.com

Printed in the United States of America

The paper used in this book complies with the
Permanent Paper Standard issued by the National
Information Standards Organization (Z39.48–1984).

10 9 8 7 6 5 4 3 2 1

To Anthony Mitchell, Johnnie Lee, Alfred Bryant,
Alejandro Vasquez, Shawn Christian, and Robert Kelly
whose support, encouragement, and faith ensured
the completion of this project.

Contents

Series Foreword

Exploring Social Issues through Literature was developed as a resource to help teachers and librarians keep pace with secondary school curriculum developments in the language arts, such as integrated studies and teaching literature across the curriculum. Each volume in the open-ended series confronts an important social issue that has both historical ramifications and contemporary relevance to high school students. The initial topics developed for the series reflect the "hot button" issues most requested by educators. Themes—such as environmental issues, bioethics, and racism—encompass a considerable body of literature. The books in this series provide readers with an introduction to the topic and examine the differing perspectives offered by authors and writers from a variety of time periods and literary backgrounds.

This resource was developed to address students' needs and appeal to their interests. The literary works selected range from standard canonical works to contemporary and multicultural adult fiction that would be familiar to teens and to young adult fiction. Many titles are found on curriculum reading lists; other considerations in selection include pertinence, interest level, subject and language appropriateness, and availability and accessibility of the text to the nonspecialist. The authors of these volumes, all experts in their fields, also sought to include a wide spectrum of works offering as many differing perspectives on the issue as possible.

Each volume begins with an introductory essay tracing the historical and literary developments related to the identified social issue. The
chapters provide brief biographical information on the writer and
present critical analysis of one or more works of literature. While the
focus of the chapters is generally full-length fiction, it is not limited to
that and may also include poetry, short stories, or nonfiction—such as
essays or memoirs. In most chapters works are arranged chronologi-
cally to reflect the historical trends and developments. In other cases
works are grouped according to thematic subtopics. The analysis includes discussions of the work's structural, thematic, and stylistic components and insights on the historical context that relates the work to
the broader issue. Chapters conclude with bibliographic information
on works cited. A selected bibliography of suggested readings that
may be helpful for further research or additional assignments is also
provided for each volume.

Educators looking for new ways to present social issues will find this
resource quite valuable for presenting thematic reading units or historical perspectives on modern problems of conflict. Students of literature as well as general readers will find many ideas and much
inspiration in this series.

Introduction

The essays in this volume address issues of race and racism as presented in novels of varying racial, ethnic, or cultural perspectives. The purpose of the following chapters is to consider both the obvious and subtle ways in which race prefigures in all facets of human life. While the focus here is mainly on impulses of racial oppression in the United States, some chapters do also transcend our national boundaries and assess the imposition of racist attitudes on foreign shores. This latter concern is of great importance because it shows how easily racist inclinations can pervade the broader society. Like a disease left unchecked, racism begins to assume a life of its own, suppressing the more natural penchant toward harmonious interaction and leaving in its wake the scarred emotional remains of a battle-weary humanity.

Any discussion of race must begin with an explanation of the difference between overt racism and institutional racism. In order for a reader to appreciate how pervasive modern-day racist impulses can be, he or she must understand how far-reaching are the tentacles of race bias. Overt racism is the most easily recognized. It operates on a personal level, whereby one individual hates another individual because of his or her racial origins or a group of individuals despises another group simply because of who they are. Some time in the past, one group decided that members (individuals) of the second group are somehow inferior. Members of the first group have created stereotypical beliefs about those in the second group. These stereotypes, having no basis in reality, begin to assume a kind of "real" status only because members of the prejudiced group insist that the stereotypes are true.

For example, in the U.S. past specifically, when whites defined blacks as being lazy, violent, or morally bankrupt, such characteristics were unfounded. Yet these whites treated blacks with disdain because they convinced themselves that blacks were thus corrupt. In typical stereotypical fashion, prejudiced whites would locate one example of an inhumane black and use that example to make a sweeping claim against all blacks. (Stereotyping is defined as using one example to draw unsubstantiated conclusions about an entire group.) Such racism is overt because those engaging in the behaviors, feeling justified and supported in their beliefs, are unabashed in their actions.

Of course, one of the most obvious examples of overt racism is European enslavement of Africans (along with the United States' rendition of that system and the post slavery enforcement of civic inequality). Clearly, overt racism is at work when an entire group of people is denied access to rights and privileges touted as defining the very core of the given society. The history of the United States (and of other countries) is one steeped in overt racism. The societal "institutions" simply supported the prejudicial beliefs of a large group of individuals. One could, in fact, suggest that historically, overt racism and institutional racism were one and the same.

As a sociological concept, however, institutional racism is synonymous with subtle racism. As such, it refers not to the traditional displays of racist behavior, but rather to the more contemporary and more obscure examples. Perhaps institutional racism is more easily clarified by the concept of the "glass ceiling." Oftentimes, in the workforce minority persons complain that they cannot advance up the corporate ladder because of institutional barriers that are not as easily identified. Such barriers are "transparent" like glass; therefore, when a minority person complains of such barriers, he or she is often accused of manufacturing ills that do not exist in the system. Work superiors suggest that he or she is not yet qualified to advance, that there are rules for advancement that must be met, and so forth. However, the minority employee has witnessed other nonminority colleagues with similar or lesser qualifications maneuver up the corporate ladder with no difficulty. The racism here is defined as "institutional" because it exists in the very structure of the corporate entity; one might even say it exists in the walls of the building, in the very culture of the organization. The minority person oftentimes cannot advance because he or she never even hears of a new position opening up until it is later filled. With institutional racism, actual rules and practices that everyone is supposed to follow are purported to exist. But what happens in reality is that certain individuals are made privy to information before the fact, and then those individuals are better poised to exploit opportunities when they arise. On the surface, the system looks as though it operates on fair principles, but in actuality it functions as prejudicially as it might have under an overtly racist regime.

Institutional racism exists because flawed individuals still control the system. For the most part, individuals prefer to work with other individuals who make them feel comfortable, and those who make them feel comfortable are those who look like them. That is a human condition most cannot deny. The problem is, of course, that when only one racial or ethnic group enjoys a position of power, then that group will welcome to its ranks only those persons with similar qualities. A minority person can never hope to advance in such a system wherein the institution becomes an extension of individual prejudice. For this reason, challenging institutional racism is much more difficult, and it requires constant vigilance and determination. As noted previously, because rules of fairness ostensibly exist, the empowered in the flawed institution become defensive because, from their perspective, if guidelines of fairness exist, then surely they are being enforced. The institution, or company, cannot possibly be acting inhumanely. People are not generally willing to critique their own prejudices, and they are less willing to acknowledge the fact that their biased attitudes have a far-reaching impact on the institutions they oversee.

Yet another issue that one must broach when addressing the topic of race is cultural bias. Quite often, individuals exhibit racist behaviors when they encounter cultural traits different from their own. But because such cultural biases are often so subconscious, individuals never confront them. To better appreciate this assessment, one must first define exactly what comprises culture. From an anthropological perspective, culture is made up of two components: (1) a deep or "core" structure and (2) a surface structure. Of the two components, the one that most specifically defines the culture is the former, hence the term "core." This component includes concepts such as beliefs, values, the quality of human interactions, and the ritual practices of a cultural group. On the other hand, the surface structure includes emblems such as dress, language, food, art forms, or any trait that an outsider notices in an immediate encounter with another cultural group. As is so often the case, cultural groups are judged primarily by these surface "trappings." And because these surface qualities clearly differ from cultural group to cultural group, an outsider observing another group will devalue the group simply because it is different from what he or she knows. Difference is equated to inferiority. Hence, someone from a majority group, in haughty fashion, might proclaim, "Between you and me, _____ has no culture." Such a statement means that the hypothetical individual from the minority group lacks "culture" because he or she is not a member of the speaker's cultural group. This statement is clearly flawed because what it fails to recognize is that every individual, as a member of some cultural group, in fact has a culture. Granted, it may differ from the dominant cultural group, but it is a culture nonetheless. This individual may dress differently, eat different foods, or speak a different language (or dialect), but he or she still has a culture. To declare that someone has no culture is an attempt to dehumanize and objectify him or her. Once one realizes, however, that what really defines culture is the deep structure (rituals, beliefs, and values), then one comes to appreciate that the quality of human interaction within a cultural group is more important than how the cultural group dresses or speaks. Do members of the "other" cultural group treat each other humanely? Do they treat outsiders humanely when they encounter them? Do they respect the natural world and its resources? The answers to these questions define the essence of a cultural group, not insignificant surface ornaments. Difference is not inferiority; difference just "is." Understanding culture and the danger of cultural bias is key in gaining a more comprehensive understanding of race and racism. Subconscious cultural biases, manifested in misunderstanding the true nature of culture, often inform racist behaviors, especially those behaviors that result in institutional forms of racism. Confronting cultural bias leads to confronting race prejudice and initiates the process of snuffing it out.

The novels analyzed in this volume confront race from different historical periods and from different racial perspectives. The chapters are categorized primarily by race (e.g., the African American perspective, the Latino perspective, the Native American perspective, and so on). Within these racial divisions, attention is given to a particular novel's placement along the continuum from overt racism to the subtlest form of institutional racism. One novel may address issues along the continuum, or a couple of novels (within a given racial category) may represent different points along the continuum. The main purpose, however, is to show how each racial group must cope with the various facets of racial oppression within a particular historical moment or at any given time.

The first group presented is the African American perspective, introduced with a chapter on Mark Twain's *The Adventures of Huckle-*

berry Finn (1885). This novel serves as an almost perfect model for understanding the complexities of racism (i.e., overt racism vis-à-vis institutional racism). This American classic provides a historical frame for showing how the overt racism inherent in legalized enslavement translates into institutional forms of racism following the Civil War. The antebellum setting of the novel is obviously the ideal context for exploring the blatant racism that has enslaved Jim simply because he is black. In short, slavery is overt racism. The key to appreciating *Huck Finn*, however, is knowing that Twain is at once exposing the obvious form of racism and unmasking the institutionalized forms rapidly emerging during the period (Reconstruction and post-Reconstruction) in which he is writing. By the time *Huck Finn* is published in 1885, the rights ostensibly afforded blacks by the 13th, 14th, and 15th Amendments to the Constitution have been negated by varying loopholes that Southern states exploit to ensure second-class citizenship for former slaves. *Huck Finn*, then, charts the emergence (within the fabric of U.S. society) of entrenched racist doctrine, as experienced by African Americans.

Continuing the analysis of the African American perspective is a discussion of Richard Wright's *Native Son* (1940) and Harper Lee's *To Kill a Mockingbird* (1960). Both novels address what is perhaps the most racially charged issue ever to confront American society: the accusation of a black man raping and/or killing a white woman. The almost moblike response to Bigger Thomas's murder of Mary Dalton in *Native Son* and to Tom Robinson's alleged, though unfounded, rape of Mayella Ewell in *To Kill a Mockingbird* reveals how even years after the publication of *Huck Finn*, the primacy of overt racism is still well established. And then when comparing *Native Son* to *To Kill a Mockingbird*, one better appreciates the pervasiveness of institutional racism. Tom Robinson's guilty verdict underscores the fact that in a racist society, black men receive no justice, and it also underscores the fact that, notwithstanding his guilt in the Mary Dalton case, Bigger was never poised to receive any justice either. Had these white communities (a jury of supposed "peers") even considered the possibility of institutionalized forms of racism, they would have had to acknowledge and then confront the social, political, and economic circumstances (which collectively collapse into a racial circumstance) that brought these two black men to the present moment of even having to face a judicial tribunal. That Bigger, and certainly that Tom, is even a defendant in such a trial, clearly suggests racialized societal collusion.

Jose Antonio Villarreal's *Pocho* (1959) and Sandra Cisneros's *The House on Mango Street* (1984) offer insights into the Latino experience, particularly from the Mexican American point of view. Each is a bildungsroman (or "growing up" text) that charts the development of the main character as he or she comes to grips with the racial implications of life. Both Juan Rubio in *Pocho* and Esperanza Cordero in *The House on Mango Street* are budding writers who view the world with the artist's keen eye. As such, they interrogate all that they see, including the restrictive boundaries of racial oppression. As young people, they recognize overt racism when it emerges, whether it comes in the form of Juan's teachers suggesting that he pursue a vocational track instead of an academic one or whether it comes in the form of Esperanza's white neighbors fleeing the community because of an increased Mexican American presence. Their main conflict, however, is internal, as they constantly wage war against attempts to make them feel inferior. Theirs is a journey about self-fulfillment and individual pursuit. Ever vigilant against the low horizons that a racist society attempts to offer them, both Juan and Esperanza understand that overt racism will succeed as subtle racism if they begin to doubt themselves. In other words, institutional racism in these two novels is identified as self-limitation. Their bodies and their minds are the "institutions" that they must keep racist-free. With the ancestral spirit of immigrant possibility, failure for these two is not an option. Whether it is Juan in the 1930s and 1940s, or Esperanza in the 1960s and 1970s, failure would be tantamount to a victory for racism. Neither is prepared to accept such defeat.

In the Native American selections, attacking racism entails embracing the natural world while dispensing with (both emotionally and intellectually) the doctrines of the so-called civilized world. Margaret Craven's *I Heard the Owl Call My Name* (1973) and Leslie Marmon Silko's *Ceremony* (1977) present the world of the dominant (i.e., white) culture as inherently racist. For the Native American characters in both novels, sustaining one's cultural primacy is the best weapon against this racism. Communing with the natural world and respecting the resources provided by a higher power, or Supreme Being, the Indian villagers in Craven's novel and protagonist Tayo in Silko's novel emerge as strong cultural beings. They understand the true concept of culture (that deep structure grounds the culture), and knowing that they are graced with unshakable beliefs and values, these characters define themselves not against the cultural norms of white society but in harmony with their own cultural space which uplifts and inspires.

The Asian American selections, Arlene J. Chai's *The Last Time I Saw Mother* (1995) and Nora Okja Keller's *Fox Girl* (2002), examine the process of gaining one's emotional wholeness by learning the truth about one's identity. Chai's novel addresses this issue from the modern-day Filipino perspective, while Keller's novel offers a mid-twentieth century Korean perspective. In both novels characters must investigate the mystery of their heritage, one impacted by the "intrusion" of mixed blood. In a decidedly racist environment, Keller's main characters Hyun Jin and Sookie struggle to survive because of their relatively darker complexions, probably the result of their mother's relationship with black soldiers. Because many of the United States-influenced Koreans are trying to be as American as possible, even in their Korean homeland, they adopt racist attitudes against anyone not noticeably "pure." For them, American whiteness is the benchmark for achievement. Any person "spoiled" by darker blood is to be shunned and oppressed. That Hyun Jin and Sookie fight to survive and refuse to deny who they are shows their bravery in combating the racist forces dominating their lives. Though they must seek an unorthodox means of survival, their manipulation of the racist system and their acknowledgment (and even celebration of their identity) confirms a victory for them and future generations. For Chai's protagonist Caridad, the victory results from her accepting the fact that she is comprised of many different parts. In her case, such variation is the result of having been given away as a baby. Her identity is shaped by both her biological and her legal parents. Caridad's multifacted persona emerges as the metaphor for the mixed-race heritage of her daughter Marla. Only when she can honor every part of her heritage can she also embrace all of the bloodlines coursing through Marla. Emotional wholeness is tantamount to racial wholeness, and racial wholeness is defined by welcoming all racial threads into the fabric.

The three remaining novels offer insights into the Italian American, Jewish American, and Jewish-Arabic perspectives: Rita Ciresi's *Sometimes I Dream in Italian* (2000), Chaim Potok's *The Chosen* (1967), and Amy Wilentz's *Martyrs' Crossing* (2001), respectively. What links the novels in this final group is the subtlety with which race is analyzed. While Ciresi's novel does expose the obvious conflict between blacks and Italians when blacks begin to move into the Italian neighborhood, it deals specifically with the more subtle form of racial oppression visited upon Italian Americans. Though considered just white in the larger context of racial politics in the United States, Lina ultimately learns that her "whiteness" does not protect her from racial or ethnic prejudice. When her German American lover wants her to speak Italian in the throes of passion, she comes to understand that she is no more to him than an exotic object, made all the more appealing because of her being Italian not because of her individuality. The complexity of race politics becomes painfully apparent to a previously deluded Lina. Potok's *The Chosen* and Wilentz's *Martyrs' Crossing* are subtle in their racial analyses because the novels conflate race conflict and religious conflict. In the former, intra-Jewish political animus (the "war" between conservative and moderate Jews) dominates the text. In the latter, Jewish-Arab contentions are highlighted. Both novels, however, expose the pain involved in individual sacrifice when the demands of group membership (racial and/or religious) deny the kind of individual compassion and camaraderie that define one's humanity. Whether two Jewish friends are kept apart because they hail from two different sects (in *The Chosen*) or whether an Arab mother is prevented from acknowledging the kindness of an Israeli soldier (in *Martyrs' Crossing*), racial-religious-ethnic prejudice undermines the humane principles that the warring groups purport to uphold.

Each of the analyses presented herein confirms the complexity of race and racism, not only in the United States, but also beyond her shores. The novels, however, also showcase protagonists bold enough to believe that the racial differences exploited historically to antagonize and segregate groups can, in fact, serve as bridges toward unity, tolerance, and compassion. Theirs is a multiracial, multiethnic, cross-cultural perspective grounded in hope rather than complacency. Reading these novels, one is left not with a foreboding sense of "race" burden, but with a renewed sense of racial wonder and possibility.

Mark Twain, *The Adventures of Huckleberry Finn* (1885)

PLOT SYNOPSIS

Episodic in structure, *The Adventures of Huckleberry Finn,* hereafter referred to as *Huck Finn,* charts the oftentimes dangerous, yet always humorous, antics of 13-year-old Huck and adult runaway slave Jim. As fugitives (Huck from his abusive father and Jim from slavery), the two travel up and down the Mississippi River seeking independence and self-identity in a world that would rather restrict them.

Important to note is the fact that the two flee only after their living circumstances change or threaten to change. At the beginning of the novel, Huck is living comfortably with the Widow Douglass, who has unofficially adopted him, and her sister Miss Watson. Though he found it difficult at first to adjust to civilized life, Huck ultimately acclimates himself reasonably well. Unfortunately, his father Pap comes along after several months and removes Huck to a spartan cabin where he imprisons the boy and emotionally and physically abuses him. Knowing he must escape, Huck fakes his own murder and ventures out, not knowing exactly where he will go.

Jim, like Huck, lives a fairly comfortable life, in spite of his slave status. The property of Miss Watson, he is admired by slaves all around for his storytelling ability and for his good nature. Jim's decision to escape is motivated by the knowledge that Miss Watson may sell him farther south to New Orleans. Horrified by that prospect, Jim decides to risk his life in an effort to achieve freedom. Unaware that the other has fled (although everyone thinks Huck is dead), Jim and Huck find each other in the woods of Jackson Island, a swath of land in the middle of the river.

From the moment Huck and Jim find each other, they remain dedicated to ensuring the other's safety. They hunt, fish, and float their canoe about the island enjoying both the freedom and the solitude. Several days later, they come upon a two-story house floating upon the river. Inside they spy a dead man, whose identity Jim does not disclose to Huck. Understanding that he needs to protect Huck emotionally and keep the boy focused on their escape, Jim relates only at the very end of novel that the dead man was Pap.

Huck reveals his dedication to Jim when he risks detection by going back to town to find out what he can about everyone's response to his "death" and Jim's escape. Dressing up as a girl and paying a visit to a longtime resident of the area, Huck discovers that a group of men are planning a late-night search of the island in an effort to capture Jim, whom they suspect to be there. Losing no time after making his discovery, Huck rushes back to Jim, warns him, and insists that they leave instantly. The two resume their nomadic life on the Mississippi.

In one of the most emotionally charged scenes in the novel, Huck and Jim lose each other in a thick fog as they fall prey to a swift river current. Separated for several hours, each fears for the other's life. However, when Huck finally finds Jim, he feigns ignorance about the fog and recent danger in an attempt to make Jim think that he has dreamed the entire event. Deceived for several minutes, Jim finally discovers the truth, whereupon he lashes out at Huck for exhibiting such dishonorable behavior. Because Jim was so worried about Huck and feared that the boy had possibly drowned, he cannot believe that Huck would play such a prank on him. After the tongue-lashing, Huck, feeling quite guilty, is forced to do something he has never done before: humble himself before a black person and apologize. An important turning point in their relationship is reached. In the scene following, Huck's dedication to Jim is confirmed when they are approached from a slight distance by a skiff. When the men aboard inquire about Jim's race, Huck assures them that Jim is his white father. When the men want to come closer to confirm Jim's racial identity, Huck deceives the men into believing that "Pap" has a contagious disease. The men quickly retreat and even give Huck money to assuage their guilt for not helping the lad further. Though Huck still harbors ambivalent moments about his assistance to Jim, his feelings of loyalty to his friend continue to outweigh any allegiance he might feel to the so-called civilized world.

Their friendship is tested time and time again, and each time Huck and Jim are separated, they pine for assurance that the other is safe. Soon after their encounter with the men on the skiff, a steamboat plunges into their raft. Huck and Jim dive off opposite sides and lose each other. Huck makes shore and soon finds himself in the care of the Grangerfords, an earnest, kind family who unfortunately are also involved in a decades-long feud with the Shepherdson clan. For the next several days Huck is welcomed on the Grangerford farm; he is even given his own slave for the duration of his stay. Though the Grangerfords treat him like he is family, Huck is elated to learn that Jim is fine and that he has been waiting patiently in the woods for Huck's return. In fact, the Grangerford slaves have been caring for Jim during this time. By now, Huck's true family is Jim.

Huck and Jim's next encounter is with two con artists who call themselves the king and the duke. Their specialty is bilking small-town residents out of their hard-earned money. For several days following, Huck is an accessory to their schemes (Jim is always left on the raft in hiding). From trying to defraud a couple of towns by performing embarrassingly poor skits from Shakespearean plays, to presenting themselves as the lost-long heirs of a recently deceased wealthy man, the king and the duke endanger Huck's life at every turn. After being run out of a few places, the two resort to the worst form of betrayal for Huck: they print up a fake "wanted" poster for Jim and then sell him to the quickest respondent. By the time Huck discovers the treachery, Jim is locked in a shed several miles away at the Silas Phelps farm.

Huck goes to the farm as quickly as possible. Because the Phelps family have been expecting their nephew (ironically, Huck's friend Tom Sawyer), they think that Huck is Tom. Not wanting to alert them to his true reason for coming, Huck does not identify himself. Knowing, however, that Tom is expected at any minute, Huck decides to go down the road a piece and intercept his friend so that they can come up with a more detailed plan of deception: Huck will continue to be Tom, while Tom becomes Sid, Tom's actual younger brother. Fully ensconced in the Phelps household, Huck and Tom devise a plan to free Jim, whom they have discovered in the shed. While Huck wants to free him at the first opportunity, Tom, consumed by his adventurous inclinations, wants the escape to be heroic and romantic and thus time-consuming.

For several days, the two boys force Jim to house pet snakes and rats, carve mythical statements in rocks, and suffer other "heroic" antics. Though Jim tires of the process, he has no choice but to play along. While Tom is fairly satisfied that his plan is materializing well, he ultimately decides that the adventure requires a bit more danger. Tom then drafts an anonymous note to Aunt Sally and Uncle Silas informing them that a gang of ruffians intend to steal the fugitive locked in their shed. Tom intends to usher Jim to freedom just at the moment when Uncle Silas and his vigilantes come to intercept.

In the ruckus that follows Tom is shot in leg, though the three make it to safety. When Huck and Jim discover that Tom is injured, they insist on securing the help of a doctor, no matter the consequence for Jim. After deciding that Jim will hide when the doctor comes, Tom and Huck agree that Huck will go in search of a doctor. After finding the local doctor and directing him to Tom, Huck goes back to the Phelps farm. The next day, Tom, the doctor, and Jim are brought back home. Jim is discovered when he comes out of hiding to assist the doctor in his care of Tom. After regaining consciousness, Tom reveals that Jim is actually free and that he has been free all along—a recently deceased Miss Watson having freed him in her will. Tom's Aunt Polly soon arrives to confirm this news. The novel ends with Tom's suggesting that he, Huck, and Jim head westward to uncivilized territory. Though Huck likes the idea, he ultimately decides to strike out by himself, without any restrictions or any obligations to others.

HISTORICAL BACKGROUND

Though set in the antebellum period, *Huck Finn* was written in the period following the Civil War. Mark Twain began writing this American classic in the summer of 1876, and he also abandoned the project during this same season, not resuming work on it until 1882. Important historical events more than likely resulted in this decision.

To appreciate more fully the national portrait of 1876, one must recall the always precarious state of black life in the United States during the 13 years prior. In the midst of the Civil War, President Lincoln endorsed the Emancipation Proclamation, which became law in 1863. Ostensibly passed to free the slaves, the proclamation, in fact, freed only those slaves who resided in Confederate states (i.e., those formally at war with the Union). Non-Confederate, slave-holding states were not affected. The fight for equal rights for blacks would continue with the passage of three significant legislative acts, known as the "Civil War" amendments to the Constitution. In 1865, the 13th Amendment officially abolished slavery everywhere. The 14th Amendment followed in 1868, and it promised equal protection under the law, regardless of race. In 1870, the 15th Amendment prohibited federal or state infringement of rights regardless of race, color, or previous servitude. It, along with the Reconstruction Act of 1867, also bestowed upon black men the right to vote. The Civil Rights Act of 1875 followed. The era known as Reconstruction extended from the end of the Civil War in 1865 until 1877. During this 12-year period, the federal government assisted in rebuilding, or "reconstructing," the South, and it also provided services to ensure the protection and the "upbuilding" of the southern black community. The Freedmen's Bureau was established to assist in these efforts. Schools were established to educate former slaves and to acclimate them to a life of independence. In 1877, however, federal intervention in southern life came to an abrupt halt.

In 1873 the country fell into depression, and, as is typical of human response to economic troubles, racial tensions mounted. Southern whites, in particular, took issue with federal assistance to black life, begrudging former slaves' access to the limited resources. Over the next three years matters worsened. The presidential race of 1876 was a contentious competition. Because Rutherford B. Hayes, a Republican, won by a slim margin, southern congressional Democrats threatened to block his certification. However, these political parties reached the famous Bargain of 1877, which declared that Democrats would support the Hayes election if the new president promised to end Reconstruction. The federal troops originally disseminated throughout the South to ensure the peace and to ensure southern adherence to the "Civil War" amendments were summarily removed, and a reign of southern terror on black life was unleashed.

That Twain would both begin and end work on *Huck Finn* in 1876 is significant. The summer of 1876 was marked by irony. On the one hand, the country marked the centennial of its independence, celebrating and hailing those famed characteristics of U.S. life: liberty, justice, and the right of the individual. On the other hand, the summer also witnessed an increase in the intimidating practices of white supremacist groups. The Ku Klux Klan was established in the winter of 1865–1866. Though it began as a prankish men's club, it soon defined itself as an organization hostile to Reconstruction efforts and Republican interests. By 1876, this group, along with the Knights of the White Camelia, the White Brotherhood, and southern Rifle Clubs throughout the South, terrorized blacks and those sensitive to civil rights.

By the time Twain resumed work on *Huck Finn* in 1882 and published it in 1885, the gains made by blacks after the Civil War were rapidly eroding. In 1883, the Supreme Court repealed the Civil Rights Act of 1875. Lynching of blacks intensified. Sharecropping, de facto slavery, replaced legalized slavery. The convict-lease system became the law of the southern land. In this system, black men were convicted of baseless crimes such as vagrancy or the "intent to steal." As convicts, they were made to work for powerful whites in much the same fashion as they would have worked in slavery.

Twain wrote *Huck Finn* during a time of great upheaval for blacks. When he first began the novel in 1876, Twain drafted it up to the Grangerford-Shepherdson episodes. In particular, he stopped writing at the point when young Buck Grangerford tries (and by most accounts, fails) to explain to Huck the rationale for the decades-old feud. Buck suggests that his family and the Shepherdsons must honor a code of chivalry established long ago. Even though the feuding is barbaric, both families believe they have a duty to uphold tradition regardless of its inhumanity. This same paradox would inform the national dialogue during the summer of 1876. The United States' longtime and current rhetoric of freedom and liberty tried to mask the fact that civil rights for blacks were soon to be eroded with the Bargain of 1877 and ensuing barbarous acts throughout the South. When Reconstruction ended in 1877, southern Democrats (those with Confederate sensibilities) began once again to control state governments. By the end of the 1880s and into the 1890s, no one would have believed that during the height of Reconstruction 2 senators and 14 representatives occupied positions in the federal Congress, while scores of other blacks held statewide offices throughout the South. Privileges gained were soon privileges lost, as new exclusionary civil laws in the South quickly superseded natural (or God-given) laws that would hold blacks as equal citizens and declare them equal to the task of holding office.

The Phelps farm sequence in *Huck Finn* offers Twain's candid appraisal of not only America's treatment of blacks during and after Reconstruction, but also the conflict between civil law and natural law. That Jim would have to endure Tom and Huck's childish antics during his incarceration at the Phelps farm, when Miss Watson has already freed him, is representative of U.S. treatment of blacks in the postbellum period. Ostensibly they are free after 1865, yet after enjoying some of the many privileges that come with freedom, not the least of which is holding public office, blacks are systematically (and legally, until proven otherwise) relieved of their rights. The pranks that Jim suffers underscore the frivolous treatment of blacks in the latter half of the nineteenth century. By natural law Jim is free, and even by civil law, Jim is free (by virtue of Miss Watson's will). Yet by virtue of the customs of the day (Huck and Tom's "customs"), he is still held in captivity because even when the civil law squares with natural law, customary law often overrides both. Likewise, after Reconstruction, certainly natural law would declare blacks as equal to whites, and even federal civil law would declare the same; however, the customs of the South, which became more forceful as Democrats assumed greater powers, mandated black subjugation. By 1896, with the famed *Plessy v. Ferguson* Supreme Court case, segregation and black civic inferiority became the law of the land. Twain clearly uses Jim's story in an effort to showcase not black buffoonery (as some have unfortunately argued) but societal and political buffoonery when used in an effort to denigrate and oppress. Using the antebellum period of legalized enslavement to critique the postbellum period of ostensible liberty, Twain shows how many postbellum and post-Reconstruction activities were designed to ensure, and often resulted in, de facto slavery.

LITERARY ANALYSIS

To fully appreciate Twain's treatment of race in *Huck Finn*, one must first understand the prevalence of irony and satire in the novel. Without question Twain ridicules the entire southern social order, and this attack on social "norms" is apparent from the beginning of Huck's story. When Huck and Tom and their friends establish their gang in chapter 2, they devise certain codes of behavior that at once mirror and mock the sacred tenets of the Southern Code: (1) respecting and protecting justice, (2) maintaining a sense of propriety or decorum, (3) embracing Christian values, (4) defending chivalry, (5) upholding the principle of noblesse oblige, and (6) honoring family loyalty. The boys draft an oath that each member of the gang swears to obey. It calls for every member to protect the gang's secrets, but if any member divulges information, another member will be ordered to kill him and his family. In addition, no nonmember can use the mark of the gang, and if anyone does, he must be sued. If he offends the gang again, he must be killed. Anyone whom the gang must kill is to be killed in a most horrific fashion. Immediately following this colorful description of the oath, Huck then states that everyone thought it to be "real beautiful" (Twain, *Huck Finn*, 8).

The discrepancy between the horrors presented therein and the members' satisfaction with the propriety of the oath underscores

Twain's attack on the very nature of a social order (represented by the boys' gang) that would uphold such hypocritical notions. On the one hand, the boys vow to protect and defend each other; yet with the first suspicion of a member's betrayal, the suspect is to be killed without the benefit of a trial (there is no real justice then). The boys think their gang is honorable and moral, but they intend to rob innocent people (propriety is compromised). The boys purport to be good Christians because they decide it would be wrong to rob people on Sunday; yet they ignore the fact that such behavior would be wrong any day of the week for a true Christian. Without question, the idea of chivalry is skewed because they protect nothing innocent and virtuous. While noblesse oblige calls for the charitable concern for those less fortunate, the gang exhibits no concern for the socially or economically disfranchised. Even though they profess a concern for family loyalty, at a moment's notice the family of anyone suspected of offending the gang can be killed. Every principle of the Southern Code is mocked as Twain takes issue with a society that uses a righteous façade to maintain its racist oppression of black slaves. The world of the gang becomes a microcosm of the slave-holding South. Further critiquing this society from the unique perspective of *Huck Finn,* one finds that notions of right and wrong and good and bad become inverted in an inherently evil society (one that upholds the "peculiar institution" of slavery). Absolutes become murky. But what has this to do with race?

As most critics agree, a crucial turning point in the novel occurs when Huck makes the ultimate decision to shepherd Jim to freedom. Though he is torn about his decision because he thinks he is committing a major social and moral offense, Huck finally decides that he would rather help his friend. So in chapter 31 Huck declares, "All right, then, I'll go to hell" (235). He has reconciled himself to the fact that if society demonizes him for his decision then he is prepared to suffer the consequences. Of course, the reader knows that Huck is acting in a morally correct fashion because he is responding to a power higher than the power exhibited in man's morally corrupt world. Since the world Huck occupies is morally bankrupt, any act considered wrong in it is actually right. Any act considered right in this world (as in oppressing blacks) is actually wrong. Twain's satire here, with its attendant irony, is quite poignant.

Reversals of definition also apply to the portrait of Jim. While some may view him as a stereotypical slave who fawns over a white boy and, as a result, compromises a strong black identity, analyzing Jim in light of the novel's ironic impulses yields an entirely different characterization. One must also remember that the novel and Jim's role in it are presented from the perspective of a 13-year-old boy who has been affected by the "civilized" society he yearns to escape. So even though, on the surface, Jim may appear to be an object instead of a man, in fact it is Huck's skewed and naive version of Jim that one sees. One must analyze Jim both within and beyond the present social context. From Huck's point of view, Jim is simply a "nigger" and a slave, and as such, he should remain inferior to someone like Huck, even though Huck, in patronizing fashion, treats Jim well. Whenever Jim presents to Huck some of his superstitious "wisdom," Huck considers it an indicator of black intellectual inferiority. However, in almost every instance, as the reader pierces Twain's verbal irony, Jim emerges as the intellectual victor. The racial tension in the novel almost always results in Jim's favor. For example, during one of Huck and Jim's seemingly insignificant exchanges, Jim informs Huck that bees do not sting idiots, a pronouncement to which Huck responds that he does not believe Jim because he (Huck) had taunted bees many times and they did not sting him. Considering himself to be Jim's superior, Huck simply knows that he is not an idiot and that Jim's belief system about bees must be flawed. However, Twain's underlying comment seems to be that Jim, superstition notwithstanding, is right and that Huck is an idiot, at least in comparison to Jim. Both Huck's naiveté and his arrogance with regard to Jim prevent him from considering any possibility other than the one that makes him racially superior. Jim, however, striving to function in this woefully unequal world, maneuvers to best Huck and the perspective he represents. Although in Huck's world, the world of slavery, black is equated with ignorance, primitivism, and the like, when one's vision is projected beyond the confines of that world and one can view Jim more objectively, Jim and blackness become equated with shrewdness, resourcefulness, and survival.

Jim's intellectual prowess is made apparent again when he and Huck discuss the biblical Solomon. Though Huck assumes that everyone would interpret Solomon's famous act in the same way (that Solomon hoped to challenge the real mother to come forward when he threatens to split the disputed baby in half), Jim defies the standard interpretation in favor of his own. Jim concludes that Solomon was not as wise as purported to be, that in fact Solomon's behavior was foolhardy. Jim maintains that because Solomon had many children of his own, he was not averse to wasting the life of one child. When Huck challenges him, Jim philosophizes that every story has a meaning deeper than the one usually offered. Huck does not accept Jim's reasoning. Instead, he dismisses Jim's interpretation as nonsensical. However, one can easily argue that Jim exhibits independent thought and that he is not easily swayed by popular beliefs. That Jim would have his own thoughts indicates that he is an agent in his life and not merely an object. Though one might not agree with his conclusions, one must respect his willingness to challenge any argument. As an independent individual, Jim is better poised to challenge other popular beliefs, particularly those pertaining to black inferiority and subservience.

That Jim has a clear sense of self and vision is evident when he shares his plans with Huck in chapter 16. As a man with plans, he intends to shape his own destiny rather than be manipulated by the whims of his "superiors." Upon arriving in the North, Jim intends to work and save until he can purchase his wife. Then together they will work and save until they can buy their children. If, however, the owner refuses to sell the children, Jim will secure the help of abolitionists and steal them. Though Huck considers Jim's plan indicative of an ungrateful scoundrel (as opposed to the good "nigger" persona Jim has presented before), Jim shows himself to be a proud husband and father who must take responsibility for his family's well-being. Slavery's racism would hold Jim in contempt for his actions. However, Jim has risen above such emotional and psychological confinement. Rather than being subdued by the racial tensions endemic to an enslaved condition, Jim exploits such tensions on his behalf. Knowing that slavery and its proponents are his enemies, Jim is unapologetic about having to "steal" what is rightfully his. He understands that what is "wrong" in slavery's world is actually "right" above and beyond that world.

In this same scene, Jim takes the opportunity to manipulate Huck a bit further and to ensure that Huck will continue to assist his efforts. Already tasting the nectar of freedom, Jim gushes his thanks to Huck, relaying to the boy that he is Jim's only true friend. Jim goes on to say that Huck is "de on'y white genlman dat ever kep' his promise to ole Jim" (99). Here Jim manipulates not only Huck, but also the very Southern Code that Huck feels guilty about not obeying. As a white (southern) gentleman, Huck is supposed to uphold the slave-holding principles of the region. However, Jim redefines the gentleman as someone who functions honorably outside the confines of the Southern Code. For Jim, to be a gentleman is to aid another human being (regardless of his race) and not impede his advancement. One could argue that Jim is also trying to teach Huck a lesson as the boy, on the brink of puberty, journeys to manhood. As a boy (white or otherwise), Huck owes Jim a certain deference simply by virtue of Jim's age. However, when the white boy becomes a man, his authority supersedes that of the black male, regardless of the age of the latter. When Jim refers to young Huck as a white gentleman, in some ways he is asking Huck what kind of white man will he be: will Huck be the usual southern white gentleman (who oppresses the black man), or will he embody true gentlemanliness and advance the humanity of all? Jim's rhetorical and intellectual maneuvers position him as the leader and the thinker; his blackness makes him in no way inferior to Huck or any of the other whites he encounters.

The tenuous and delicate nature of black-white relations is presented in a section of the novel that seems immaterial to race issues. However, one particular scene in chapter 18 is vitally important in its revelation about the importance and necessity of black defense strategies during any black-white encounter. After Huck has been separated from Jim during the Shepherdson-Grangerford escapades, the two are reunited when Jack, the black youth assigned to Huck, tells Huck to follow him into the woods to look for snakes. After escorting Huck to a certain point, Jack instructs Huck to continue on the path a bit farther where he will locate the reptiles. Huck soon discovers Jim in a previously undisclosed location. Not completely ignorant of Jack's methods, Huck says to Jim: "If anything happens, *he* ain't mixed up in it. He can say he never seen us together, and it'll be the truth" (124). Even at a young age, Jack understands that he must behave in a way to protect himself, not just in the present moment, but also in the future, and he must never exhibit any kind of knowledge in the presence of whites. During his encounter with Huck, he never mentions Jim's name nor does he mention that a slave is hiding in the woods. By not voicing information, he is ostensibly unaware of any pertinent information. In this way, "ignorance" is protection; it is not the reality of the black mind. The bizarre nature of race relations demands that someone like Jack feign ignorance, when he is perhaps the smartest in the group.

BIBLIOGRAPHY

Chadwick-Joshua, Jocelyn. *The Jim Dilemma: Reading Race in Huckleberry Finn.* Jackson: University Press of Mississippi, 1998.

Doyno, Victor. *Writing Huck Finn: Mark Twain's Creative Process.* Philadelphia: University of Pennsylvania Press, 1991.

Egan, Michael. *Mark Twain's Huckleberry Finn: Race, Class, and Society.* London: Chatto & Windus, 1977.

Fishkin, Shelley Fisher, ed. *A Historical Guide to Mark Twain.* New York: Oxford University Press, 2002.

_____. *Was Huck Black?: Mark Twain and African-American Voices.* New York: Oxford University Press, 1993.

Foner, Eric. *America's Unfinished Revolution, 1863–1877.* New York: Harper & Row, 1988.

Fredrickson, George M. *The Arrogance of Race: Historical Perspectives on Slavery, Racism, and Social Inequality.* Middletown, CT: Wesleyan University Press, 1988.

Mensh, Elaine, and Harry Mensh. *Black, White, and Huckleberry Finn: Re-imagining the American Dream.* Tuscaloosa: University of Alabama Press, 2000.

Twain, Mark. *The Adventures of Huckleberry Finn.* New York: Penguin, 1985; originally published in 1885.

2

Richard Wright, *Native Son* (1940)

PLOT SYNOPSIS

Bigger Thomas, a 20-year-old youth from Chicago's Southside, is offered an opportunity to work for a wealthy family who live in Hyde Park, the more affluent area of town. Because he needs to support his mother, brother, and sister, Bigger feels compelled to accept the job, even though he is less than eager about the situation. But when the department of social services threatens to curtail its assistance to the family, Bigger knows he must work. Accustomed to loafing about with his three friends (committing petty thefts and other misdemeanors), Bigger has never before had any major responsibility.

The major plot action is set within a three-day period, from Saturday morning to late Monday night. On Saturday morning, when the novel opens, the Thomas family is presented in their forlorn condition: a rat-infested, one-room dwelling ill-equipped to accommodate four people. Living in such circumstances, the Thomas family has no alternative but to urge Bigger to take the job with the Daltons. Though he is not to report for duty until late in the afternoon, Bigger leaves the apartment so that he will not have to hear his mother recite all the reasons why he must take the job and why he must do nothing to sabotage his new chances.

Bigger goes in search of his three friends, with whom he is planning to rob a neighborhood business. Even though Bigger is afraid to rob a white business, he does not want to appear cowardly in the presence of Gus, Jack, or G.H. After their initial meeting, the four intend to reconvene later in the afternoon and conduct their robbery, during a time when the business is free of customer traffic. Minutes before the appointed time, everyone arrives except Gus. Bigger uses Gus's delay (Gus is not even late yet) to initiate an argument to thwart the robbery attempt. Angry and frustrated because he is firmly aware of his fear (he thinks he has hidden the fear from his friends), Bigger prepares for his crosstown journey to the Dalton home.

Early that evening Bigger reports to the Dalton mansion to assume his new duties as the family chauffeur. After meeting Mr. and Mrs. Dalton, who both welcome him, Mr. Dalton establishing ground rules and expectations, Bigger is left to acclimate himself to his new surroundings. Later in the evening he is slated to drive the Daltons' daughter Mary to a lecture at the university.

At the appointed hour, Bigger leaves the house with Mary. He tries to gauge what is expected of him, in terms of behavior and interaction with his new employers. Bigger soon learns that Mary is not attending a lecture but is instead meeting her boyfriend, Jan Erlone. After he picks up Jan, Bigger is instructed to drive the two to the black Southside where they can find authentic "black" food and atmosphere. Bigger is uncomfortable when Jan and Mary treat him like a friend and not an employee. He is reluctant to join them for dinner and drinks, but they insist. When some of Bigger's acquaintances see him socializing with whites, he is embarrassed and somewhat humiliated.

Upon leaving, the three drive around while Mary and Jan continue to drink and flirt with each other in the back seat. Just before they return to the Dalton home, Jan exits the car, with the assurance that Mary is safe with Bigger for the remainder of the trip. Bigger delivers Mary home near 2:00 A.M. on Sunday morning, but when they arrive, he realizes that she, now fully intoxicated, cannot find her way into the house and to her room. He then accompanies her to her quarters, all the while fearful that they will be discovered and that he will somehow be blamed for everything that transpired.

Finding his way to her room, Bigger deposits Mary on the bed. Moments later, the blind Mrs. Dalton enters the room to check on a now incoherent Mary. Because he does not wish to be discovered in what might be considered a compromising situation, Bigger attempts to suppress the subtle noises that Mary is making. He places a pillow over her head, and in the following moments when she squirms for release, he presses the pillow even harder. Finally, she relents, and Bigger releases her. All the while, Mrs. Dalton calls out to Mary. By the time Mary is silenced, Mrs. Dalton is satisfied that she is resting comfortably, albeit intoxicated.

After Mrs. Dalton departs, Bigger comes to face his worst nightmare: Mary is dead. A black man is responsible for the death of a white woman. Now completely confused, Bigger places Mary's body in a trunk and drags it out of the room and down to the basement. He places the corpse in the furnace, only to find that it is too long to fit in completely. Determined to dispose of the evidence, Bigger severs Mary's head, tosses it into the furnace, and repositions the body.

After disposing of any other evidence, Bigger returns to the apartment he shares with his family and tries to steal a few hours of sleep. Because he was originally scheduled to drive Mary to the train station on Sunday morning, along with a packed trunk (the same one he used to transport her body), Bigger goes back to the Dalton home with the intention of "carrying out" these duties, as though nothing amiss has occurred. Because he knows that Mr. and Mrs. Dalton sleep late on Sunday and because Mary is supposed to be away for a couple of days, he believes that he has some time to think about his next action. After delivering the trunk to the station, Bigger returns to the Dalton house, goes to his quarters, and relaxes there until he is called.

Later Sunday afternoon the Daltons discover that Mary never arrived in Detroit. Assuming initially that she may be up to some of her youthful antics, the Daltons try to ease their apprehensions about their daughter's well-being. They send Bigger to the station to retrieve the trunk, and they hire a private investigator to pursue the matter. In the midst of the excitement, Bigger manages to sneak away to visit his girlfriend Bessie Mears. While he is hesitant to admit everything to Bessie, he does share with her the money he pilfered from Mary's purse. He tries to convince Bessie to engage in a ransom scheme with him, whereby they will try to extort funds from the Daltons by claiming that they have Mary. Without fully convincing Bessie of this plan, Bigger returns to the Dalton house in the evening, this time to be questioned more fully by private investigator Britten.

Bigger concocts a story that incriminates Jan, telling the private investigator that Jan accompanied Bigger and Mary back to the Dalton house and that Jan, Mary, and he then went to Mary's room. He concludes by stating that he was asked to transport the trunk to the basement in anticipation of the next morning's journey. According to Bigger, that was the last time he saw Jan or Mary. After his questioning, Bigger is allowed to leave. He returns to Bessie's, where he, much to Bessie's disenchantment, prepares a ransom note. Bigger goes back to the Dalton house and slips the note under the front door without discovery.

Soon after Mr. Dalton reads the note, the entire household is aflutter. Bigger continues to act as innocent as he can. Later into the night, once news has leaked out when Jan is brought into police headquarters for questioning, reporters advance on the scene and insist upon an interview with Mr. Dalton. After a while, housekeeper Peggy instructs Bigger to empty the ash bin from the furnace. When he hesitates to do the job properly, one of the reporters intervenes to help him. In the process some of the ashes are thrust to the floor. When the reporter begins to examine the contents more closely, he discovers bits of bone and also an earring. As other men close in to have a look, Bigger steals away unnoticed and then flees.

Running away to Bessie's, Bigger forces his girlfriend to escape with him. Because he is concerned that the authorities will search for him either at Bessie's or at his mother's apartment, Bigger and Bessie remove to an abandoned building. Reconsidering his situation, however, Bigger decides that he can neither take the completely unnerved Bessie with him nor leave her behind to divulge what she knows to the police. Believing his only alternative is to kill her, Bigger bludgeons the innocent woman with a brick and deposits the body in an airshaft during the early morning hours of Monday.

After daylight, Bigger is a man on the run. The entire Southside is cordoned off with widespread police presence. Authorities and volunteers search every building, occupied and abandoned. Going from one location to another, Bigger tries to avoid capture. Ultimately, however, he is chased up a water tower. Police must force him down by instructing firemen to turn the fire hoses on Bigger. Torpedoed with rushing streams of water, Bigger submits on Monday night.

Though Bigger finds himself in the worst possible trouble that a black man could face, he is offered legal assistance from one of Jan Erlone's friends. Boris Max, a Jewish attorney who supports Communist causes, agrees to defend a now completely despondent Bigger. Putting forth his best effort and a unique legal strategy (arguing about the race and class implications of Bigger's case), Max works tirelessly to save Bigger's life. Not surprisingly, the court chooses to impose the death penalty. By the novel's end, though, Bigger has come to respect Max and his genuine concern for the less fortunate like Bigger. He must now await his legal fate.

HISTORICAL BACKGROUND

Published in 1940, *Native Son* addresses, in part, those racial tensions prevalent during the 1930s, both in the North and in the South.

One important social phenomenon that helps to frame the text is the Great Migration. Following World War I, scores of southern blacks moved to northern urban centers in search of greater economic and social opportunities, all the while hoping to rid themselves of overt racial traumas too well-known in the South. While looking to the North as some kind of Promised Land, many blacks became disheartened by the squalid conditions they found there. Urban poverty was more pronounced than the conditions they had known in the South, where even under the sharecropping system (or de facto slavery) they could plant and grow food, eking out a meager existence. In the North blacks found that their living arrangements were just as circumscribed as they were in the South. Even if they could afford better circumstances, they were denied access. Jim Crow was as much alive in the North as it was in South.

The Thomas family history mirrors this typical black migratory experience. During his conversation with Mary and Jan in the Southside restaurant, Bigger reveals that his family has been in Chicago for only five years, having come there from Mississippi. He also states that his father was killed back in Mississippi years earlier during a riot. And while the details of this event are left sketchy, Jan's follow-up questions would suggest a racial overtone to the unfortunate killing. Having suffered, then, from typical southern racial hatred (with the loss of a husband/father), the Thomas family comes to Chicago to forge a better life. The opening scene of the novel would suggest, however, that their attempts have been thwarted. When Bigger is forced to hunt down a huge rat and bludgeon it in the presence of not only his younger brother, but also his mother and sister, the reader is left with a vivid and permanent image of urban economic inequity.

Still another significant event that informs *Native Son* is the trial of the Scottsboro Boys, the infamous 1931 case wherein nine black youths were tried for allegedly raping two white women in Scottsboro, AL (See Historical Background in Chapter 3). This case highlighted the worst form of racial tension between blacks and whites, as it exposed southern whites' most deeply entrenched social fear: black male encroachment on the white female body. The various trials and appeals, which proceeded throughout the 1930s and 1940s, are newsworthy throughout the time Wright is writing *Native Son*.

Both the Scottsboro case and the impetus for black migration serve as the ideal context for *Native Son*. While the court case reminds readers of the racial threat on black men in the presence of white female accusation, black migration reminds them as well that blacks often departed the South to escape widespread lynch practices, which often resulted from false accusations lodged against black men. When Bigger Thomas finds himself in the clutches of the justice system, the crime about which the community is most horrified is not the murder, but the alleged rape of Mary Dalton. Even though Bigger is far removed from the South and even though he does not rape Mary, the mere allegation stirs racial tensions and heightens mob hysteria more completely than in any southern place. There is a real irony in the fact that Bigger finds such trouble in a northern locale, when perhaps one of the reasons his family moves to Chicago is to avoid such trouble, especially given the violent end suffered by his father. Now 20, Bigger left the South at 15, maybe with his mother's hoping that they were leaving before Bigger became a perceived threat to white womanhood.

Still another important event contextualizes *Native Son*. And while it does not initially seem to have racial significance, ultimately the infamous Loeb and Leopold murder case, as referenced in the novel, does contribute to the overall discussion of race. On May 21, 1924, 18-year-old Richard Loeb and 19-year-old Nathan Leopold, sons of 2 affluent Chicago families, kidnap and murder Bobby Franks, a young boy with whom they are acquainted. After disfiguring the body with acid, they dispose of it in a drainage culvert. The two return to the Loeb house where they burn Franks's clothing in a basement fire. Then they notify the Franks family and attempt to extort ransom funds, claiming that young Bobby is unharmed. Before the ransom transaction is executed, police discover the body and thwart the second crime. After a long trial (or really a hearing, as the two entered guilty pleas) with a particularly impassioned defense, Loeb and Leopold are given life sentences.

Bessie alludes to the case when she reminds Bigger that the Daltons reside in the same neighborhood where the Loebs lived, Bessie having worked in the vicinity in the past. From Bessie's brief account of the case, Bigger decides to seek ransom funds from the Daltons. The real-life Loeb and Leopold case is linked then to Bigger's emerging fictional case. Herein lies the racial significance. Loeb and Leopold are not only extremely wealthy, but also intellectually advanced. Their commission of a heinous crime confirms the fact that acts of violence are not the sole purview of the socially, racially, or economically downtrodden. Loeb and Leopold stab Bobby Franks with a chisel, disfigure his body (to obscure any signs of sexual molestation, so the prosecution claims), and then deposit it in a culvert. They commit this crime for no reason other than the amusement of executing the perfect crime.

Wright is deliberate in the comparisons he draws between this case and Bigger's case. Bobby Franks's body (stabbed and disfigured) suffers more than one type of trauma, as does Mary's body (asphyxiated, decapitated, and burned). An incriminating piece of evidence is found at both crime scenes. Leopold's glasses are found near Franks's body, while Mary's earring confirms that it is her remains among the ashes on the basement floor. Loeb and Leopold's act of burning Franks's clothes in a basement fire mirrors Mary's body being burned in the basement furnace. Loeb and Leopold are suspected of having molested Franks; likewise, Bigger is accused of raping Mary. In short, both crimes are beyond human comprehension. One is committed by affluent young men whose successful future has already been determined, while the other is committed by a troubled black youth who is still trying to establish the best course of action for a minimally stable life. In drawing links between the two crimes, Wright acknowledges the human potential for inhuman behavior. However, prosecutor Buckley would have the community believe that Bigger's crime is committed in large measure because of his "apelike" inclinations. That is, Bigger's race (gender, as well) becomes almost a sufficient cause of his crime: he is a black male; therefore, he is a murderer. The Loeb and Leopold case, then, serves as more than a minor historical allusion. Further investigation of that notorious crime, while not mitigating Bigger's horrific offense, does mitigate the alleged racial cause of the crime.

A sociohistorical movement influential in the early twentieth century also addressed in *Native Son* is Communism. This phenomenon emerged with great momentum in the United States on the heels of World War I. The Communist Party of the United States of America (CPUSA), as it was named in 1929, became particularly attractive during the Depression years, staking its greatest claim on U.S. politics and labor between 1930 and 1945. Because Richard Wright flirted with Communism during the 1930s, it is no surprise that Communism would figure significantly in *Native Son*. In theory, Communists disdained capitalism, believing that the latter dehumanized society by creating and maintaining a firmly entrenched class system. Communists claimed to believe in a classless society that would allow no private ownership of property. Instead, the community would own property, and everyone would share and share alike. Ostensibly, these U.S. Communists believed that such equality and fellowship should extend across racial lines. For their beliefs, Communists, or Reds as they were disparagingly called, were considered a threat to mainstream U.S. ideals.

Because Bigger has surmised that Communists are suspect in U.S. society (capitalist Henry Dalton is pitted against Communists Jan Erlone and Boris Max), he tries to incriminate the local Communist party in the false kidnapping of Mary Dalton. Bigger makes the mistake, however, of thinking that "Reds" are as despised as blacks. While prosecutor Buckley and private investigator Britten certainly abhor Communist activity and supporters, they are still motivated more by racial animus than anti-Communist inclinations. This is evident in the line of questioning Buckley pursues when interrogating Jan about his last night with Mary. Each very subjective question is concerned more with accusing Jan of advancing social equality among blacks and whites (particularly white women and black men) than with establishing an accurate portrait of Mary's final hours. In almost every question, Buckley refers to Bigger as "that Negro" or "the drunken Negro" whom Jan left alone with Mary with no apparent consideration for her safety. While Communism, as such, is a problem and a nuisance, Communism that advocates race equality has committed the worst possible social infraction. By the time Bigger's case is adjudicated, Jan is transformed into another of Bigger's (the evil black male's) victims, his Communist leanings notwithstanding. And Mary, Bigger's most obvious victim, is forgiven for her Communist flirtations. Racial fear supersedes the Communist threat.

LITERARY ANALYSIS

Perhaps the most compelling issue presented in *Native Son* is the pervasiveness and circularity of race prejudice. One result of the comprehensiveness of such bias, as argued in the novel, is the necessity of shared guilt for Bigger's crime. Because race prejudice against someone like Bigger permeates society, he thinks he is left with little recourse other than to perform what ends up being a murderous act. Given white society's historical fear of the black male presence, Bigger knows that he cannot be discovered alone with a white woman in her private quarters. So even though he is not at fault for having escorted Mary to her room, he firmly believes that he will be blamed for something awry if he is found there. That he finds himself in Mary's room because he is trying to protect both her and his job would be a weak argument he thinks, if Mr. or Mrs. Dalton should suddenly appear.

Trying to assist Mary while also trying to respect the established race code, Bigger finds himself in an impossible situation. On the one hand, he should not be alone with Mary in this fashion. On the other hand, it is his duty as an employee to offer his assistance. Social rules dictate both realities. Therefore, when Bigger tries to silence Mary by placing the pillow over her head (in a gesture he thinks will protect him and not bring harm to Mary), he is acting by prescribed social mandates for black-white interaction. Society, with its fear of black male and white female interaction, all but forces Bigger to protect himself in Mary's bedroom. While it is true that society would maintain he should not be there in the first place, it also holds him responsible for Mary. Acting out of this sense of responsibility, Bigger is caught in an untenable and paradoxical situation.

Bigger's story highlights what has been a major irony in black-white relations since the antebellum era. While there are clearly defined rules of social segregation between blacks and whites, there is also the unspoken reality of domestic intimacy which then blurs the boundaries. Bigger, like many who function in the role of servant, becomes privileged quite quickly to many intimate details about the lives of his employers. However, like those black employees, servants, or slaves who preceded him, Bigger is expected to act as though he has no knowledge of such details. Regarding the lives of his employers, Bigger is simultaneously immersed and marginalized. When Mr. and Mrs. Dalton question him about Mary's actions and deceptions on the night of her "disappearance," they try to do so circumspectly, even though all parties concerned know that Bigger knows more than the social code will allow him to reveal. Those like Bigger are expected to see and not to see, to know and not to know. And even though the social rules (as established by white society) force Bigger Thomas to dissemble in this fashion, these same rules and this same white society blame only him when tragedy ensues. *Native Son* forces the reader to confront these subtleties of black-white interaction.

Perhaps one of the most startling revelations in the novel concerning Bigger's marginalized state is presented ironically during Bigger's brief encounter with both Mary and Jan. The zealous Communist and his girlfriend purport to have Bigger's best interest in mind. They fancy themselves champions of blacks in general, claiming their desire to unite blacks and whites to effect positive social change. When they instruct Bigger to take them to a black restaurant and when they insist that he join them in dinner and drinks, Mary and Jan present themselves as Bigger's social equals and not his superiors. However, during the conversation at Ernie's Chicken Shack, Mary, in particular, reveals her ingrained sense of superiority. Divulging to Bigger that she wants to meet other blacks and learn more about them, Mary, in the same exchange, states that she must come to know them because "they live in our country" and "in the same city with us" (Wright, *Native Son*, 70). As liberal as Mary may think she is and as socially conscious as the Daltons may think they are, Bigger knows that he is still in the midst of white people whose authority and interest can shift at will. Much later, when Max questions Bigger about his time with Mary, Bigger has to admit: "Maybe she was trying to be kind; but she didn't act like it. To me she looked and acted like all other white folks" (325). For Bigger, the Daltons are first and foremost white (their liberal inclinations aside), and as such, he sees his interaction fraught with as much danger as would define his interactions with someone as overtly prejudiced as prosecutor Buckley.

As a means of exploring the race question more broadly, Wright employs in *Native Son* the literary phenomenon Naturalism. Popular at the end of the nineteenth century and the beginning of the twentieth century, Naturalism applies the principles of scientific determinism to literature. It holds that human beings are influenced by two major forces: socioeconomic determinism and biological determinism. The former maintains that human beings are shaped by their environment (for better or worse), while the latter insists that human beings are driven by certain innate urges (e.g., hunger, fear, libido) over which they have little control and which they do not fully understand. In a Naturalistic work of fiction, oftentimes the setting is a city which is depicted as an indifferent, if not hostile, environment (a "jungle" even) where only the strongest "animals" survive.

Wright is very deliberate in his appropriation of Naturalistic elements. From the opening scene of the novel, when Bigger is forced to chase and then slay the rat, to other moments when Bigger is described as existing in a jungle or being moved by a force he cannot resist, Naturalistic characteristics abound. In *Native Son* Wright does not use Naturalism to present Bigger as an animal by virtue of his racial or ethnic composition (though such an argument is espoused by Buckley and supported by the angry mob). Instead, Wright uses Naturalism to describe a state of affairs when a human being (in this case, a black one) finds himself trapped in a world where he can exercise few, if any, choices.

Race is certainly at issue here, but not in terms of Bigger's race being a cause of his behavior. Rather, race is at issue because Bigger finds himself restricted and "caged" because he is black. Early in the novel, when Bigger and his friend Gus spy an airplane overhead, Bigger fantasizes about the opportunity to fly an airplane himself. But he knows that race restrictions deny him the chance. The choices left for him seem to be no real choices at all. He can either work for the Daltons or suffer having welfare subsidies curtailed for his family. In other words, his needs (food and shelter) are threatened if he does not accept the job. Working, then, to satisfy only biological (or basic) needs, without any immediate consideration for other aspirations (symbolized in the lofty heights achieved by the airplane), Bigger functions like an animal who must use his instincts in this attempt at survival. Unlike Mary Dalton, who can choose either to attend a lecture at the university or to socialize with Jan, Bigger has no such options. Every move he makes is to protect himself.

Not surprisingly, the prosecution depicts Bigger as an animal because he is black. Buckley acknowledges no motive for Mary's death other than Bigger's vile nature. Unwilling to consider Bigger's need for self-preservation (not wanting to be discovered by Mrs. Dalton), Buckley simply uses race prejudice to make his case. According to Buckley, all upstanding white men should strike at the opportunity "to crush with his heel the woolly head of this black lizard" (373), an argument made, ironically, after Buckley expresses regret that race and class have been made an issue in the hearing. While Buckley wants the court to believe that Bigger is an animal because he is black, the defense suggests that Bigger's circumstances, which have left him "cornered" and "frightened," compel him to respond in the only way that threatened beings do: acting to verify that well-established, if tacit, principle—self-preservation is the first law of nature.

On the other hand, the defense recharacterizes Bigger's act in light of the larger social context. In an elaborate argument, Max explains the painful reality of black-white relations in the United States. According to Max, because the white community has, in large measure, satisfied its own advancement at the expense (in fact, the very degradation) of the black community, in a kind of zero-sum game (whites advance when blacks suffer), any resistance within the black community to such inequality is perceived as a threat to whites. Therefore, insists Max, not only Bigger's actions, but also his very existence "is a crime against the state" (367). Even Bigger understands that he "committed rape every time he looked into a white face" (214). For Max, a black person who simply wants to be is problematic for the larger white community. It stands to reason that when one defines one's success on another's failure, when the other begins to reject inferiority, then one feels immediately exposed and vulnerable. The historical state of black-white relations and race prejudice render the black person as a perceived threat; there is no inherent, or natural, trait that so positions him or her.

BIBLIOGRAPHY

Bloom, Harold, ed. *Bigger Thomas*. New York: Chelsea House, 1990.

Bowser, Benjamin P., and Raymond G. Hunt, eds. *Impacts of Racism on White Americans*. Thousand Oaks, CA: Sage Publications, 1996.

Dawahare, Anthony. *Nationalism, Marxism, and African American Literature Between the Wars: A New Pandora's Box*. Jackson: University Press of Mississippi, 2003.

Hodes, Martha Elizabeth. *White Women, Black Men: Illicit Sex in the Nineteenth-Century South*. New Haven, CT: Yale University Press, 1997.

Hutchinson, Earl Ofari. *Blacks and Reds: Race and Class Conflict, 1919–1990*. East Lansing: Michigan State University Press, 1995.

Leopold and Loeb Murder Case official Web site, "History," Marianne Rack-liffe (2000-2004), www.leopoldandloeb.com (accessed November 2, 2003).

Majors, Richard, and Janet Mancini Billson. *Cool Pose: The Dilemmas of Black Manhood in America*. New York: Lexington Books, 1992.

Richard Wright: Black Boy, "Biography," www.itvs.org/RichardWright/index.html (accessed November 2, 2003).

Steinberg, Stephen. *The Ethnic Myth: Race, Ethnicity, and Class in America*. Boston: Beacon Press, 2001.

Woodward, C. Vann. *The Strange Career of Jim Crow*. New York: Oxford University Press, 1974.

Wright, Richard. *Native Son*. New York: Perennial, 1998; originally published in 1940.

3

Harper Lee, *To Kill a Mockingbird* (1960)

PLOT SYNOPSIS

This novel is a bildungsroman (a work that charts the development of a young character from innocence to experience). Narrated by adult Jean Louise Finch (known as Scout), the novel details events from Scout's life during the period, 1933–35, when she is six, seven, and eight. Scout spends much of her time with older brother Jeremy Atticus Finch (or Jem) and, during the summers, with their friend Charles Baker Harris (or Dill), who visits his aunt, a neighbor of the Finch family.

Scout and the boys occupy their time by observing the people of Maycomb, Alabama, and learning the mores of small-town southern life, while also becoming aware of human frailties and shortcomings. As their mother has died, Scout and Jem are raised mainly by black housekeeper Calpurnia, a woman who takes her job seriously and who is supported unconditionally by the children's father, Atticus Finch.

When the novel opens, Scout is reminiscing about a series of events that have forever changed the lives of the Finch family. The summer before Scout begins school, she and Jem meet Dill for the first time, and that encounter marks the beginning of the transformation. At Dill's urging, Jem and Scout agree to venture next door to the Radley house, a strange place made even more mysterious by the fact that the Radley son, Arthur (or Boo), now an adult, has not been seen in years. Because Jem and Scout consider the house as almost haunted, they have always shied away from it. When Dill prompts them to trespass in an effort to flush Boo out, Scout and Jem, though unsuccessful, are set on a journey that prods them to test other boundaries as well.

At the beginning of the school year, when Scout enters first grade, she finds herself immediately at odds with her teacher. A precocious child, Scout has already learned to read and to do some writing. Rather than being pleased, a miffed Miss Caroline insists that this mastery, which she blames on Atticus (though in reality Calpurnia has performed much of the instruction), has made Scout almost unfit to teach. Unintentionally, Scout is once again pressing boundaries. Her father encourages her to learn how to get along in the world without causing too many disturbances. The remainder of the school year progresses with little difficulty.

By the next summer, when Dill returns for his annual visit, Jem and Dill distance themselves from Scout somewhat. While they still play with her on occasion, they also reject her spontaneously and without provocation. As the boys mature, Scout must find her own way of coping and growing. Sometimes she spends time in the kitchen watching Calpurnia cook; at other times she socializes with Miss Maudie Atkinson, an eccentric neighbor who treats Scout like an adult and respects the young girl's curiosity. Two significant occurrences impact Scout's perspective during this particular summer. One is that while rolling inside a discarded tire (pushed by Jem and Dill), Scout lands in the Radley yard. Before she can free herself and flee, she hears laughter emanating from inside the house. This marks a bit more intimate contact with the Radley inhabitants. And then, just before Dill leaves for the fall, the three of them venture into the Radley yard at night, once again with the hope of getting a peek at Boo Radley. On being frightened away by old Mr. Nathan Radley, Jem loses his pants when they are caught in the fence. Later that night, he decides to go alone and retrieve them. When he refuses to allow Scout to accompany him, Scout finally realizes that she and Jem will no longer be as close as they once were. Jem is becoming a man who increasingly considers Scout an immature child.

Strange occurrences visit the Finch neighborhood during the following school year. Now in the second grade, Scout has never before witnessed such a harsh winter. When it begins to snow, she is horrified, thinking that the world is coming to an end. Days later, Scout is awakened suddenly in the middle of the night when her father informs her that Miss Maudie's house is on fire. Joining others standing on the street watching the men haul Miss Maudie's furniture away, Scout is mesmerized by the spectacle. She does not realize it when someone stealthily places a blanket around her. Once the excitement subsides and Atticus notices the blanket, everyone realizes that Boo Radley must have wrapped the covering around Scout. Season by season Boo is becoming less monstrous and more human to Scout and Jem. During this same time, Scout learns that Atticus will be defending Tom Robinson, a black man accused of raping a white woman. Already Scout is being harassed at school because of her father's involvement in the case. Nevertheless, Atticus insists that Scout not allow others to rile her because of their ignorance. The Robinson case serves as the focal point for the second half of the novel. Scout and Jem are exposed to the subtleties of black-white race relations in the South.

Tom Robinson is tried during the summer following Scout's second-grade year. Now eight, Scout considers herself wiser and more courageous. Late on the night before the trial begins, Scout accompanies Jem and Dill when they go in search of Atticus, whom they find standing guard at the jailhouse. Just as they are about to approach, a gang of men arrive to confront Atticus and to seek vengeance on Tom. The three children, much to Atticus's surprise and disenchantment, rush to Atticus's side whereupon Scout, in a seemingly naive maneuver, begins to shame the men, one of whom she recognizes as the father of one of her classmates. Within minutes, the crowd disperses, and Atticus escorts his protectors home.

At the trial the next day, Jem, Scout, and Dill sneak into the courthouse and make their way to the balcony where they sit with the black spectators. After Robert Ewell testifies that he saw Tom Robinson attempt to rape his daughter Mayella, the alleged victim gives similar testimony. Tom provides a different accounting of events, and his point of view is supported by the fact that his physical disability prevented him from possibly beating Mayella. As Tom's left arm is useless, the injuries that Mayella sustained on the right side of her face could not have been caused by Tom. When Jem hears the testimony, he is certain that Atticus has won the case. Scout, however, in an attempt to understand all of the ramifications of the case, has not been so convinced.

The jury returns late in the evening of this one-day trial with a guilty verdict. Though it is obvious to everyone that Robert Ewell beat his daughter after he discovers that she has made advances toward Tom, the all-white, all-male jury still convicts the innocent man. As Scout details, Jem is stunned by the result. He cannot understand, given the overwhelming evidence, how Tom could be found guilty. Dill is sickened by the entire experience, while Scout remains concerned about what all of this means for the future. A few days later, when Robert Ewell threatens Atticus, Scout begs her father to secure a gun for his protection. Unfazed by the threat and the request, Atticus insists that he cannot change his pacifist ways because of someone like Robert Ewell. His choice serves as yet another lesson for the children.

The Robinson tragedy is exacerbated when days later Tom, in an attempt to escape, is shot and killed by guards. Those closest to Atticus are as stunned as he is. Jem cannot even discuss the trial or any ensuing events, and Scout does not understand how hate can penetrate a society so thoroughly. Later in the fall, to bring some stability and positive excitement to the community, the women of Maycomb decide to stage a Halloween pageant. On the night of the affair, when Jem and Scout are returning home in complete darkness, they are stalked by someone later to be revealed as Robert Ewell, who is still angry at Atticus for embarrassing him on the witness stand. A scuffle ensues, and Robert Ewell is stabbed. Jem, injured in the scuffle, is spirited away toward home by someone else who suddenly appears. Scout, regaining her senses, follows the two home. Jem is left unconscious but well. Scout soon discovers that Boo Radley rescued Jem. The quiet and shy Boo allows Scout to befriend him, though he remains completely silent. By the novel's end, the sheriff convinces Atticus that Ewell fell on his own knife, even though both he and Atticus know that Jem stabbed Ewell in self-defense. Though Atticus does not want a judicial cover-up, the sheriff insists that he simply will not pursue the matter. A sleepy Scout is put to bed, and Atticus awaits Jem's recovery in the morning.

HISTORICAL BACKGROUND

Published in 1960 in the throes of the Civil Rights Movement, *To Kill a Mockingbird* is directly influenced by the social tensions of that era, while it is also influenced by the tensions of its 1930s setting. The focal point of the novel, Tom Robinson's rape trial, hearkens to that signal event from 1955, which many consider to be the impetus for the modern Civil Rights Movement. In August 1955, 14-year-old Emmett Till was lynched in Money, Mississippi, after allegedly flirting with a white woman. When Emmett's mother Mamie Till exposed her son's badly disfigured body to the media, the South's shame was exposed to the world. By December 1955, when Rosa Parks defended her right to sit anywhere on a Montgomery, Alabama bus, the spirit of civil rebellion was fully realized.

In the 1930s, another famous case received national attention, that of the Scottsboro Boys. In 1931, nine black youths were tried in Scottsboro, Alabama, on charges of raping two white women. Originally found guilty and sentenced either to death or life in prison, ultimately the U.S. Supreme Court reversed the convictions and remanded the cases to the lower courts for retrial after several years. In 1937, charges against four youths were dropped; a fifth youth was released in 1938. The cases of the others extended into the 1940s. Each of them lost many years of productive living while in the clutches of the justice system. Tom Robinson's fictional case occurs in the midst of this actual case. The Scottsboro trials anticipate and confirm the judicial travesty that awaits an innocent Tom.

To Kill a Mockingbird captures the raw emotion associated with historical black male, white female interaction. From southern white society's perspective, black males posed a threat to the purity of southern womanhood and should, therefore, be feared, monitored, and kept at bay. From the black perspective, white females posed the more dangerous threat because any accusation from a white woman would result in assured death for the black male. This tension-laden reality defined black/white relations for the 300 years prior to the novel's publication. Because of the gravity of Tom's alleged crime (given this historical truth), the novel is fraught with tension at crucial moments in the plot. Probably the most emotionally charged moment (in terms of a potential for violence) is presented when the Cunningham-led mob comes to lynch Tom on the night before his trial. The scene is made more frightful because Jem, Scout, and Dill are also witness to what could occur. Though Scout succeeds in shaming the Cunninghams, the circumstance could have easily turned violent and even deadly.

While the novel is set in the mid-1930s, it is affected by the mid to late 1950s era of its actual composition. This period of change is clearly anticipated in the novel. Even the period following the 1960 publication is anticipated. The 1950s and 1960s witnessed racial upheavals, which had never before been known. From the bus boycotts of the late 1950s to the marches, sit-ins, and resultant bombings and retaliations of the early 1960s, black America had decided that, no matter what, the time was ripe for change and that the status quo was no longer acceptable. Blacks wanted the right to vote, and they wanted the civic responsibility of jury duty (so that miscarriages of justice like that witnessed by Tom Robinson would become less frequent). The possibility of such change filters into *To Kill a Mockingbird*. Atticus makes this abundantly clear when, in trying to explain to Jem and Scout why usually reasonable white men could render such an unreasonable verdict, he prophesies a new day to come. For him, all of the unfairness is "adding up," and one day "we're going to pay the bill for it" (Lee, *To Kill a Mockingbird*, 221). The day that Atticus envisions is the volatile 1950s/1960s context.

Another interesting historical truth addressed in the novel is the time-honored social order, both racial and economic. At the top of the hierarchical structure are the wealthy whites, who rule by virtue of their race and their economic might and whose sole function is to protect a social system that upholds their power. Other less affluent whites occupy spaces beneath the very wealthy, while blacks and poor whites function at the bottom of the system. The social myth suggests that the wealthy maintain a charitable attitude, or noblesse oblige, toward those less fortunate. In reality, the powerful create a hostile environment whereby poor whites and blacks fight each other and remain blinded to the real source of their oppressed circumstance. Poor whites, who have blindly accepted the notion of white supremacy, still believe that their white skin affords them privilege; thus they channel their hatred toward blacks whom they consider inferior. Blacks, who believe poor whites practice intimidation and violence through the Ku Klux Klan, are socialized to despise poor whites; yet blacks often fail to realize that all behaviors allegedly exhibited by the Ku Klux Klan are allowed only insofar as they are sanctioned by the rich and powerful. So while blacks treat poor whites as "trash," they forget that poor whites are exploited by affluent whites who truly treat them as "trash," something disposable (used for the dirty work of violence and intimidation and then discarded).

To Kill a Mockingbird exposes these myths in the presentation of the Ewell family and in Atticus's repeated assessments of certain issues. Though all the other whites in Maycomb despise the Ewells and consider them beneath contempt, they use the Robinson trial and the Ewells to uphold the myth of white superiority. Even though the Ewells are not respectable people, their whiteness (when the sanctity of white womanhood is at stake) affords them some protection against perceived black encroachment. When the system protects the Ewells in this instance, they continue to feel superior to blacks, and the blacks hate them even more because once again whites have benefited at the expense of blacks. The conflict between poor whites and blacks is sustained, and the system (orchestrated by the affluent for their special benefit) continues to function largely unhampered. Atticus, however, pierces the mythology and disrupts, at least within his own family, the long-held belief in upper-class white superiority. Once again in conversation with Jem and Scout, Atticus deconstructs the system when he redefines "trash." Instead of considering it to be a description of the downtrodden whites, Atticus defines "trash" as any white man who would knowingly cheat a black man, regardless of the white man's economic status. In this regard, then, Atticus is disparaging those in control of the social, political, and economic system who deliberately oppress black people. What has been accepted as historical truth becomes historical myth, and actual truth is unearthed.

The period in which the novel is set also provides a context for exposing other forms of social hypocrisy. In this mid-1930s era, Adolf Hitler is subjecting Jewish people to innumerable atrocities, all in the interest of protecting Aryan purity. Scout is learning about these ills in school, and while she sympathizes with the victims abroad, she is even more horrified that the sympathies extended by other whites in her community are not also extended to the plight of blacks who are also her neighbors. That the same teacher who criticizes Hitler for his practices would also justify the outcome of Tom Robinson's trial puzzles and offends Scout.

The mid-1930s setting of the novel serves, as well, as an ironic context for analyzing black-white relations. In the throes of the Great Depression, many of the citizens of Maycomb are struggling to survive. The Cunninghams are so poor that once when Atticus assisted the family patriarch with a legal matter they had to pay him by offering vegetables and other goods harvested from their farm. Likewise, after Atticus defends Tom, many in the black community show their gratitude, not by paying Atticus with money but by delivering goods to the house. With everyone struggling so desperately, reason would suggest that everyone work together and pool resources, regardless of race or perceived station in life. Yet racial and other tensions of the era prevail and prevent real human cooperation.

LITERARY ANALYSIS

Scout, Jem, and Dill learn a harsh lesson about U.S. race relations, particularly in the South. Even though the overwhelming evidence indicates that Tom Robinson is innocent of rape, the fact that he is a black man accused of such a crime by whites makes him guilty, regardless of reason and logic. The issue of black-white relations is a muddled and complex one that the three children try desperately to

understand. One of the overarching themes in the novel is the appre-
ciation of different perspectives. The lesson that Atticus tries most
often to impart to a curious and precocious Scout is the importance
(in fact, the necessity) of considering a given issue from the opposing
party's point of view. Understanding that racial interactions, or confrontations, often result at best in an impasse and at worse in violence,
Atticus knows that in order to achieve even a modicum of progress
one faction must consider the perspective of the other.

Such a lesson Atticus teaches to Scout when she has one of her first
major confrontations outside the Finch household. While this conflict
does not involve race, Atticus's response to the situation lays the foun-
dation for the kind of teaching he will use when racial tensions do
arise. When she goes to first grade, very early in the novel, Scout finds
herself at odds with her teacher Miss Caroline, who is perturbed that
Scout can already read and write. Believing Scout to be almost unfit
for professional instruction, Miss Caroline informs Scout that she
must tell Atticus to cease his reading lessons (though, in fact, it is
mainly Calpurnia who is responsible for Scout's scholastic accomplishments). A miffed Scout relays this information to Atticus who, instead
of condemning Miss Caroline for what could be considered her anti-
intellectual stance, suggests that Scout consider Miss Caroline's point
of view. Miss Caroline, according to Atticus, probably harbors no ill
will for Scout; instead, she is simply trying to teach in the only way she
knows how (by instructing her charges at the same pace with no attention to individual levels of accomplishment). As a compromise, Atticus states that he will continue to read with Scout each night if she
promises not to reveal this decision to Miss Caroline, and he admonishes Scout to get along with her teacher as best she can. Atticus
knows that Scout will make more headway with Miss Caroline if she
tries to understand her, or at the very least, Scout will suffer less stress
if she can appreciate the fact that Miss Caroline's motivations are, for
the most part, honorable (at least, in Miss Caroline's opinion).

That Scout has learned her lesson well, if only subconsciously, is
made apparent on the evening when she, along with Jem and Dill,
shames Walter Cunningham into disbanding his mob and prevents the
men from harming both her father and Tom Robinson. The Cunningham mob have come to lynch Tom before his trial, and for them,
Atticus is just a minor obstacle (and object) in their path. However,
when Scout recognizes Cunningham as the father of one of her
schoolmates (and one whom she and Jem once invited home to
lunch) and speaks to him as one individual to another, she forces him

to see not only her, but also her father as a human being. In that brief moment, Cunningham is compelled to consider the situation from Atticus's perspective, ultimately realizing that Atticus, as the honorable man Cunningham has always known him to be, is simply performing his duty as a man and as an attorney.

No matter what the situation, Atticus always tries to consider the opposing point of view. After the trial, when Robert Ewell threatens Atticus's life and spits in his face, Atticus responds with dignity and grace. In explaining his response to Jem, Atticus once again insists that his son try to appreciate Ewell's point of view (what Atticus calls walking or standing in his shoes). Because Atticus stripped Ewell of all credibility when he examined him on the stand, Ewell is angry and humiliated, and his only recourse seems to be to strike out at Atticus, who would rather Ewell exact his frustrations on him than visit them upon one of Ewell's innocent children. By considering Ewell's anger and feelings of hopelessness and also by considering even more damaging possibilities, Atticus salvages his own humanity and prepares himself, with greater fortitude, for future confrontations with Ewell or anyone else. For Atticus, "standing in the shoes" of others does not entail condoning their behavior; it means simply understanding another core of humanity in the desire to improve the human condition.

Yet another important unifying theme is finding similarities among unlikely entities. In a novel that exposes racial tensions to a great extent, locating shared qualities in circumstances that strive only to highlight differences is thematically provocative. To prepare the reader for an analysis of the similarities that exist across racial lines, the novel presents the notion of similarity in a minor character exposé. During the spring before Tom's trial, Scout and Jem, at Atticus's insistence, are forced to spend time reading to Mrs. Dubose, a terminally ill woman with a hostile disposition. She criticizes Atticus for defending a black man accused of such a horrid crime, and she also berates Atticus for the way he is raising his children. Still, Atticus insists that the children perform their civic duty and devote some of their free time to her emotional care. Upon her death, Atticus explains to Scout and Jem that Mrs. Dubose was a courageous woman. Though she had been addicted to morphine, she weaned herself from it before her death and suffered physically as a result. She was determined to die without being dependent on any substance or any person. Atticus considers her courageous because even though she knew she was already defeated (by the terminal illness) she was determined to fight anyway. That very description applies to Atticus himself, who is determined to fight on Tom's behalf even though he suffers the ridicule of many in the community and even though he knows he will not win the case, given the reality of southern justice. Linking Mrs. Dubose (a woman who seems to despise Atticus) to Atticus underscores the importance of seeking and forging bonds in seemingly incompatible situations.

Such a comparison anticipates the comparisons made between blacks and whites, especially when Jem and Scout accompany Calpurnia to her church. Though the children notice subtle differences (as in the lack of hymnals), they are most amazed at the similarities: the taking of the offering and, most captivating, what seems to be the same sermon they hear regularly at their own church. Though Calpurnia, representative of her black community, leads a separate and distinct life when not in the employ of the Finches, it is still a human life, and as such, it is not the absolute antithesis of white life. This point is made poignant when Scout and Jem come to realize Calpurnia's aspirations. She is a skilled reader who has made sure that her children can also read (evident in her eldest son's leading the hymns in church). Just as Atticus insists that Scout attend school (though oftentimes Scout wishes otherwise) and just as Atticus spends time developing Scout's reading skills, Calpurnia, too, has devoted time to the intellectual betterment of her family. Such aspirations are not black or white; they are human, and they unify humanity, regardless of race.

Just as aspirations link blacks and whites, so do certain frustrations. As Calpurnia's lesson to Scout and Jem reveals, all people become frustrated with life circumstances. When the children ask Calpurnia why she does not use standard English (which she knows very well) when addressing members of her own community, Calpurnia informs Jem and Scout that people, in general, are not comfortable interacting with someone who knows more than they do. Out of respect for their sense of security, Calpurnia finds it unnecessary to showcase her intellectual prowess. Until others want to learn more, there is little anyone can do to change them, concludes Calpurnia. The blacks to whom Calpurnia refers are similar to the whites who resist change (represented by those who despise Atticus for defending Tom). What the novel conveys is that in each race one finds those who willingly welcome progress (social, intellectual, and so forth) and those who resist it vehemently. Important to note as well is the connection made between the two themes. At the same time that her observation links the races, it also highlights Calpurnia's willingness to view the situation from the perspective of others (or to "stand in their shoes"). She appreciates the frustration felt by the illiterate blacks when they are confronted by someone who can read and speak properly. Because she understands the people, she, like Atticus, tries not to aggravate the situation any more than is necessary.

Perhaps the most pressing theme is the importance of taking an ethical stance. Though Atticus is faced with the most difficult case of his career, he accepts the challenge fully. While it is clear that he will lose, he is still determined to take a moral stand, if for no other reason than to teach his children how to be good citizens. Taking his duties as a father quite seriously, Atticus knows that he cannot instruct his children to distinguish between right and wrong (and to try to do what is right) if he is not willing to do likewise. Atticus wants Jem and Scout to understand the unfairness of a system that treats blacks differently from whites. His goal is to prepare them for the harsh realities without their falling prey to bitterness or to the disease of prejudice. As Atticus explains, "This case, Tom Robinson's case, is something that goes to the essence of a man's conscience—Scout, I couldn't go to church and worship God if I didn't try to help that man" (104). Even though Atticus's conscience stands at odds with the majority white opinion in Maycomb, he must still courageously abide by his own dictate. Though Tom's case is a futile one, Atticus hopes that he is planting a seed for progress in the next generation.

Atticus's goal is highlighted thematically by the novel's title. Wanting to sustain good in society by fighting for justice (even if it is elusive at present), Atticus believes he is acting in concert with Christian teaching and in opposition to evil or sin. The phrase "to kill a mockingbird," as presented in the novel, refers to the superstition which holds that killing such a creature is a sinful act. Because the mockingbird's sole purpose for existing is to sing (or to bring beauty), destroying it is an act of evil. Rather, the mockingbird should be protected. In attempting to bring justice to Tom Robinson and in striving to sustain the humanity of his children (in the face of so much evil and injustice in the world), Atticus is metaphorically protecting the mockingbird.

BIBLIOGRAPHY

Campbell, Bebe Moore. *Your Blues Ain't Like Mine*. New York: Putnam, 1992.

D'Angelo, Raymond. *The American Civil Rights Movement: Readings and Interpretations*. New York: McGraw Hill/Dushkin, 2000.

Hudson-Weems, Clenora, and Robert E. Weems, Jr. *Emmett Till: The Sacrificial Lamb in the Modern Civil Rights Movement*. Boston: Bedford, 1996.

Lee, Harper. *To Kill a Mockingbird*. New York: Warner, 1982; originally published in 1960.

Litwack, Leon. *Trouble in Mind: Black Southerners in the Age of Jim Crow*. New York: Knopf, 1998.

Martin, Waldo E., Jr., ed. *Brown v. Board of Education: A Brief History with Documents*. Boston: Bedford, 1998.

Royster, Jacqueline Jones, ed. *Southern Horrors and Other Writings: The Anti-Lynching Campaign of Ida B. Wells, 1892–1900*. New York: St. Martin's Press, 1996.

Rubin, Louis D., Jr., et al. eds. *The History of Southern Literature*. Baton Rouge: Louisiana State University Press, 1985.

Smiley, Gene. *Rethinking the Great Depression*. Chicago: I. R. Dee, 2002.

Sullivan, Patricia. *Days of Hope: Race and Democracy in the New Deal Era*. Chapel Hill: University of North Carolina Press, 1996.

4

Jose Antonio Villarreal, *Pocho* (1959)

PLOT SYNOPSIS

Pocho, a bildungsroman novel, charts the life of Richard Rubio, a Mexican American youth who is developing into a young man and reconciling his American self with his Mexican heritage amid some racialized moments. Episodic in structure, the novel presents key moments in Richard's life during the 1930s, when he is thrust a step further toward manhood. The main plot of *Pocho* opens in 1931 and concludes in 1940 when Richard is 18.

The only son of Juan and Consuelo Rubio, Richard is treated with special care. His mother lavishes all of her attention on him, while all but ignoring her daughters. And Juan, though not wanting to spoil the boy, finds particular joy in watching his heir develop. A somewhat precocious child, Richard is curious about everything around him. He bravely questions all information, often to the consternation of his mother, whose inability to answer sufficiently the boy's many questions leaves her feeling inadequate and insecure. Still, Richard continues to be inquisitive about all subjects.

As the novel opens, the nine-year-old boy is returning from his first confession, an encounter that has left him confused. Richard explains to his mother that the priest posed some seemingly innocent questions to him, but then the priest erupted into anger with Richard's answers. The priest asked if Richard ever played with his sister Luz or if he ever played with himself. The naive Richard, thinking that the priest is referring only to child's play and blinded to the sexual implications of the questions, answers affirmatively that he has played "alone" and with his sister. After making Richard say 50 Our Fathers and 50 Hail Marys for penance, the priest sends the boy home to rethink his evil ways. While explaining this to Consuelo, Richard suddenly realizes exactly what the priest meant; he remembers experiencing a sexual encounter with some older girls. He realizes, as well, that he misled the priest in his confession (he has not "played" with Luz, nor has he played with himself in that way). Nevertheless, Consuelo is horrified to learn that her little boy is now aware of the ways of the world; already he is growing up too fast.

Two other ensuing events push Richard farther along on his journey, each one addressing a different aspect of what Richard calls the "mystery" of life. With the first, Richard witnesses his mother suffering through labor pains as she prepares for the birth of the next Rubio child. Hearing Consuelo's moans and cries, Richard initially thinks that his mother is going to die (he even thinks that he is being punished for some bad behavior). In his naivete, Richard does not fully understand the reproductive process; yet his precocity reveals to him that every major life change (even a positive one like the birth of a child) comes as a result of major sacrifice and heartache. The second event is the death of a neighbor. When don Tomas dies, Richard is thrust into a somewhat painful reality: that the moment before death is no different from the moment after death. Life slips away so easily, and that truth frightens the boy.

The lessons Richard learns about these "mysteries" are made all the more poignant because fragile Mexican life is increasingly precious to him. As there were few Mexican families living in Santa Clara during this time, Richard, picking up the signals from his parents, realizes that no single Mexican existence can be taken for granted. For this reason, Richard takes special pleasure in accompanying his father when the older Rubio treks about visiting friends in the surrounding community. Richard's sense of identity is shaped when he witnesses these moments of heartfelt camaraderie. His commitment to heritage is fortified even more when his father allows migrant Mexican families to pitch tents in the backyard. Embraced by these families, Richard becomes completely enamored of the impromptu fiestas and Mexican songs. As more Mexicans arrive, a sense of community forms, and Richard emerges as a more secure being. While he has always exhibited endurance against such schoolmate taunts as "Frijoley bomber" and "Tortilla strangler" (47), he now has the confidence that extends from group membership. In his preadolescent state, he warms to the security.

In addition to his emergent racial consciousness, Richard also gets a lesson in class consciousness. Disenchanted with their employment conditions, migrant workers in the area decide to strike if farmers do not pay them what they consider a livable wage. On one morning when Richard accompanies his father to the Jamison farm (where Juan has worked before), father and son find a group of men demanding an increased wage from Mr. Jamison. When the farmer refuses, the men refuse to work. Moreover, they prevent the passage of any trucks to and from the orchards. When one truck collides with another, chaos ensues, and the scene erupts into a miniriot. Richard witnesses Victor Morales, a young man whom Richard immediately admires, bludgeon to death a man who struck Victor's elderly father. Later, when he is questioned by authorities, Richard, the only one who observed the crime, reveals nothing. In that one moment, Richard is pressed a little closer to the painful realities of adulthood. He and Victor now share a secret and a bond, and Richard, never betraying the trust, will no longer be the same. The ultimate irony is that the laborers end up working for the original wage that Mr. Jamison was offering. Even after the strike and the senseless death, the economic circumstance, the class warfare, is the same. Richard's innocence is on the wane.

In the next phase of his development, Richard establishes his first friendship with a girl. Mary Madison, Protestant and white, has moved to the area with her parents and brother. A couple of years younger than Richard, she is the only other student who actually uses the library and reads books. With Mary, Richard begins to share his innermost thoughts, desires, and ambitions. She respects his feelings, and he respects hers. Unfortunately, Mary's mother, who thinks all Catholics are heathens, is horrified that she has befriended a Mexican boy, and even though Mrs. Madison allows Mary to visit Richard's home, she is upset to learn that Mary ate Mexican food and that she borrowed a book from the boy. Still, Mary's father encourages Mary in her budding friendship with Richard. As a result, Mary and Richard continue to share ideas and literature, providing for each other an intellectual outlet in an otherwise anti-intellectual domestic environment.

As Richard approaches age 12, he begins to think more about what he owes to himself, instead of his responsibility to his family. When his mother informs him that he will probably never attend college because he will have to work for his family, Richard, while respecting his mother's assessment, refuses to relinquish his dream. He holds hope that the future will present to him choices that at the moment seem elusive. Richard's detachment from his family is solidified when he realizes that the family dynamic is changing. His mother is becoming less submissive to her husband, as she assumes more Americanized notions of gender equality. Though Richard understands his mother's transformation, he despises the impact such a change potentially has on his father. He realizes that the domestic order is being disrupted by his mother's emergent independence. Consuelo, who once ignored Juan's marital transgressions, now confronts Juan about his alleged affairs. She now wants Richard to report to her on his father's actions, reminding her son that as an American wife she has certain rights. Consuelo even threatens to report Juan to authorities if he ever strikes her again. Because Richard feels that this American way of life will emasculate his father and almost kill him, the younger Rubio refuses to spy on Juan. Though he may inform his mother of his father's encounters, he will do so only because he thinks his father has nothing to hide. He even tells his mother that he believes his father has a right to act in any way he chooses. With this pronouncement, Richard decides that he can no longer become emotionally involved in his parents' marital disturbances: "Whatever differences his parents might have would affect him, but they would not concern him" (Villarreal, *Pocho*, 95).

As Richard approaches 13, he spends more time with his friends, including Italian American Ricky Malatesta, Japanese American Thomas Nakano, tomboy Zelda, and even Mary Madison's brother Ronnie, whom no one really likes. Associating with this unusual group, Richard comes to learn more about himself. He learns to appreciate difference even more; rather than judging people on the basis of which racial group they belong to, Richard rates people on how they respond to him or on how they aspire to grow and develop in the same way that he does.

After Juan buys his family a new house and after they become more middle class in their values, the Rubios begin to disintegrate as a unit. Though Richard understands that changes are inevitable, he is still saddened to see the family lose some of its traditional practices. His mother and sisters are now more outspoken, as they defy the male presence more overtly and more passionately. Richard now spends more time away from home because he despises the almost palpable domestic tension. Even though he fights to protect his own individuality, he hates that his family is losing its Mexican identity and its Mexican sense of value and family loyalty. Richard's feelings are contradictory. On the one hand, he wants his family to retain group identity; while on the other hand, he is adamant in his need to formulate and then protect his separate identity.

By the novel's end, Juan, no longer feared or honored as he once was, decides to leave his family. Richard agrees to defer his own dreams in order to fulfill the newly imposed patriarchal role. However, he soon awakens to the fact that if he does not flee, he will be pressed into familial responsibility forever, possibly suffering a lifetime of regret for not pursuing his goal of a college education and a life as a writer. As the American engagement in World War II approaches, Richard decides to enlist in the navy, in the hope that he will escape the circumstances of his family life and achieve his dreams. In short, he flees so that he might live.

HISTORICAL BACKGROUND

Much of what informs Richard's devotion to and respect for his Mexican heritage lies with Juan's past in Mexico long before Richard's birth. In his younger days, during the Mexican Revolution, Juan served in the army of Pancho Villa, the Mexican revolutionary who fought fairly consistently from 1910 until 1920 against corruption and dictatorship in the Mexican government. Villa supported social and political reform. In particular he advocated a redistribution of land from the rich to the peasants and the right for all citizens to freely elect their representatives. The entire first chapter in *Pocho* focuses on Juan's move from Mexico to the United States after Villa's death in 1923. The purpose of this chapter is to provide the historical context for the 1930s racial and cultural conflict in the novel.

Losing his hero, Juan comes to the United States a somewhat defeated man, whose only desire in life is to return one day to Mexico and reclaim the honor he once enjoyed as an expert soldier and horseman. He imparts to his family his need to be a strong, virile Mexican man, who validates himself by first creating and then providing for and protecting a large family. His sense of identity is linked to his machismo and to the production of Mexican offspring, especially his son Richard. Juan despises the fact that the Spaniards control his homeland, and he is particularly offended at the way the Spaniards have "contaminated" the Mexican blood via miscegenation. He takes pride in what he considers his pure Mexican blood. To be Spanish is to be corrupt and oppressive; to be Mexican is to be authentic, wholesome, and responsive to the needs of the downtrodden, according to Juan. The older Rubio, who served in the Mexican Revolution from his late teens until his twenties, has been shaped by the spirit of revolt and by the presence of Pancho Villa.

It is this model of Mexican manhood and strength that Richard is expected to emulate. From his earliest recollection, Richard gets the message that he is to hold himself at variance with anyone considered a Spaniard. Even among his schoolmates, a determined animosity is sustained between the Mexican children and the so-called Spanish children. One particular older guy is always mean to Richard, and when Richard inquires about the hostile treatment, the guy "told him because he [Richard] was Mexican and everybody knew that a Spaniard was better than a Mexican any old day" (41). Still, there appears to be a love/hate relationship between the two groups. Consuelo states, with a modicum of pride, that Richard has Spanish blood coursing in his veins by virtue of her lineage. Her boast underscores the peculiar nature of race relations, especially between two groups whose relationship is based largely on the oppressor/oppressed model. Though the Mexicans ostensibly hate the Spanish for historical colonization, some Mexicans, like Consuelo, are proud still to be linked to the particular body in power. The strange nature of this Mexican/Spanish relationship is echoed in the novel when Richard and Juan attend a community meeting about employment conditions. Juan insists on sitting with the Spanish men because even though they are not the best people, they (according to Juan) do speak the language of Christians. In this space, the Mexicans and the Spanish find a common ground, if only temporarily. This tenuous détente highlights the fact that when two "combatants" confront other "foreign" competitors, they forge an immediate alliance. The Mexicans and Spanish, when in the presence of American blacks and poor whites (also present at the meeting), interact with each other, at least superficially in a posture of self-interest. The strange and paradoxical nature of race relations is exposed once again.

This history of the Mexican migrant worker in the United States provides an important context for considering *Pocho*. The exploitation that Juan and other men in the community suffer in the 1930s is inextricably linked to the former treatment of Mexican laborers. Great numbers of Mexican workers came to the United States between 1880 and 1890 to help in the construction of railroads. When the Mexican Revolution intensified following 1910, more Mexicans sought opportunities in the United States in agriculture, service positions, and industry. Labor conditions were often unsatisfactory, if not completely inhuman. The history of Mexican workers in the United States is fraught with examples of economic abuse. Workers complained so extensively that in 1920 the Mexican government sought to establish a

contract with the U.S. government that contained the kind of guaran-
tees outlined by Article 123 of the Mexican Political Constitution.
This contract ordered U.S. ranchers to allow workers to bring along
their families during the contract period. Purportedly no worker was
allowed to leave Mexico without a contract, signed by an immigration
official, which specified the rate of pay, work schedule, place of employment, and other related conditions. Still, abuses continued.

Perhaps the one historical phenomenon that shapes the period of
the novel's publication (1959) is the Bracero Treaty of 1942
(amended in 1943). With the increased need for laborers during
World War II, the United States sought to fill this employment gap
with workers from Mexico. The Bracero Treaty remained in effect
until 1963. In the first year, over 4,000 so-called braceros (skilled migrant workers) entered the United States. In 1956, four years before
the publication of *Pocho,* the United States witnessed its highest rate of
bracero immigration, over 445,000. Clearly, this sociological phenomenon is registered in the concerns presented in the novel. The
corrective measures that the Bracero Treaty attempts to enforce are
largely in response to the kinds of problems Juan and the other men
expose in their community meetings. The Bracero Treaty serves supposedly to protect Mexican workers not only because of their immigrant status, but also because of their racial and cultural identity.
Because Mexican workers often faced the same kinds of racist abuses,
physical and emotional, that southern blacks faced, they needed, at
the very least, some written protections. One of the key provisions of
the Bracero Treaty stipulated the following: "Mexicans entering the
United States as result of this understanding shall not suffer discrimi-
natory acts of any kind in accordance with the Executive Order No.
8802 issued at the White House June 25, 1941." Still, Mexican workers often found themselves ostracized simply for their racial difference.

Pocho chronicles an important period of Mexican American history,
from the crucial Mexican Revolution to the post-World War II explosion of Mexican immigration. The novel ends with Richard's joining
the navy just as the United States enters World War II, at the beginning of the "Bracero" period that will extend through the time period
when the author is crafting the novel. *Pocho* invites the reader to consider the plight of the Mexican American, not just during its immediate 1920s and 1930s setting, but also during the period beyond the
narrative scope of the novel.

History becomes the vehicle for considering race dynamics. The
legacy of pride and cultural responsibility that Richard inherits from

his father makes him respectful of the cultural and racial space of others. While the novel centers on the Mexican experience in the United States, the experience of others is not objectified in the process. Richard welcomes friendships from Italian American Ricky Malatesta, Japanese American Thomas Nakano, European American Mary Madison, and others. Richard embraces the beauty of difference. As a budding writer with the innate artist's eye, he sees difference as the most natural of concepts. For him, race need not inspire conflict or fear. Instead, race and race history become the means of understanding and celebrating the fullest humanity.

LITERARY ANALYSIS

The dominant theme in *Pocho* is the right of the individual to live on his or her own terms. Richard's main struggle as he wends his way through adolescence involves the universal conflict between the individual and his responsibility to the community (in Richard's case, the community is represented by his Mexican heritage which exacts certain expectations). By virtue of his heritage, Richard is supposed to uphold the Mexican tradition of unwavering devotion to family. As the only son in the Rubio family, he must assist in the care of his immediate family until such time when he marries a woman of Mexican descent and produces the next generation of Rubios. Nevertheless, even though Richard "saw the demands of tradition, of culture, of the social structure on an individual,...he was...resolved that he would rise above it" (95). Even non-Mexicans whom Richard encounters insist that he remain racially committed and that he dedicate his life to some Mexican cause even though he is not sure there is still such a cause, "at least not in the world with which he was familiar" (175). In Richard's world, he must achieve the goals he has established for himself, not those imposed from his family or from any other source. His desire to attend college and to become a writer is the only goal to which he feels any particular allegiance.

However, what makes his devotion to individual desire more problematic is the racial pressure (i.e., racism) he suffers from outside his Mexican community. Considered by many to be no more than a dirty Mexican, Richard faces the same kind of racial hatred that many members of a given minority group suffer. On one occasion, when Richard, later as a teen, is cruising around with some of his friends, they are stopped and arrested by the overzealous police. Fully aware of the authorities' intention simply to intimidate, Richard also knows that his group, comprised of a diverse body, is harassed only because Richard, a Mexican, is present. Richard's life experience has taught him that he will face such intrusions on his civic rights.

Overt prejudice is presented also when Mary Madison's mother criticizes Mary's desire to befriend Richard. Because Richard is different, practices a different religion, and honors different cultural practices, Mrs. Madison questions his desirability not only as a neighbor, but also as a companion for her daughter. When Mary brings home a book she has borrowed from Richard, Mrs. Madison insists that Mary leave the "dirty" book outside. Mary, however, echoing Richard, states that "no matter how dirty the pages were, the words on them made them like clean" (77). Mary and Richard have come to understand that, in fact, "one can't judge a book by its cover," just as one cannot judge a human being by his or her appearance or ethnic difference. The words inside the book represent its soul (which is far more important than its cover), just as a human being's actions give truth to his spirit more so than his outward look. Mexican Richard and European Mary work to heal the very wounds that the social order, represented by Mrs. Madison, would rather expose and aggravate. The intellectual space (as symbolized by the book they share) that Mary and Richard carve out shuns the narrow and restrictive categories of human interaction designed merely to oppress and dehumanize.

Richard has faced this social order time and time again during his academic journey. Well-meaning school counselors have often advised him to pursue a vocational track instead of a collegiate one. According to such advisors, in order for Richard to be a good and happy Mexican, he should take auto mechanics or welding. That he would take advanced courses seems a completely foreign concept to the counselors. Richard sees these low expectations as part of the "unwritten code of honor" (108) that deliberately stifles (or attempts to stifle) the aspirations of those like him. It seems as though all of society (represented by Mrs. Madison, the police, and even school authorities) colludes to ensure Richard's individual failure.

Race in this novel functions in a particularly disruptive way. On the one hand, Richard's Mexican community (family) wants him to dedicate his full life to it because he should feel a racial and cultural allegiance. Yet, Richard wants to be his own person, racial responsibility notwithstanding. On the other hand, the external world (represented by white, Protestant U.S. society) lumps Richard in with all other "dirty" Mexicans, none of whom should aspire to the American dream and all of whom should feel lucky simply to exist in the United States. In both of these circumstances, race has the potential to circumscribe Richard's actions. If he adheres to family and community wishes, he will not realize his full potential. If he succumbs to the biases of the larger society, he, too, fails himself. Both factions want Richard, in essence, to isolate himself from the mainstream world. What is potentially problematic is that Richard, in feeling family pressure and in tiring of societal browbeating, could erupt in a decidedly militant stance and become so consumed with so-called Mexican pride that he would lose sight of his individual goals.

As Richard matures, he comes to realize that he must be leery of all self-proclaimed authority figures. He learns that American culture, in particular, is replete with subliminal messages designed to make him feel inferior. Once when he is discussing horses with his father, Richard intimates that white horses are, of course, superior to brown ones. Juan, once an avid horseman, relays to his son that American movie propaganda would have him believe so, but that, in fact, the color of a horse does not determine its superior nature. From such lessons, Richard will bravely challenge the opinions of others and question their motivation. Already an avid reader who seeks his own information, Richard is less easily duped by his teachers' appraisal of events. He even considers most of his teachers stupid because they know no more than he does. Still, without succumbing to militancy, Richard links a healthy Mexican pride with his own brand of individuality to form a healthy self-image. He is both artist (budding writer) and Mexican American. Neither identity lessens the other. Richard comes to the conclusion that no matter what happens in life and no matter the response of others, everything always comes back to how he feels and responds to a given situation. For him, simply *being* is important, not being something or someone for the good of the social order; and since he already *is,* he has no one to be concerned about, with regard to self-identity, self-actualization, or self-image, other than himself.

What both saves and inspires Richard is his delving, at a young age, into both epistemological and ontological questions. The former addresses the origin of knowledge, while the latter ponders the issue of existence. Regarding epistemology, from the moment Richard leaves his first confession, he struggles with the question of who decides what knowledge is, as well as the ensuing question of how knowledge is then organized and disseminated. Though he cannot quite articulate the importance of these questions, Richard understands on some instinctual level that whoever controls the scope of knowledge also controls the power. From deciding on what is important, to deciding how terms and labels are defined, to determining which terms, labels, and definitions are superior or inferior to others, the brokers of knowledge control that state of the world (or that unwritten code that Richard will forever challenge). By interrogating his world in this way, Richard challenges his racial position in the U.S. epistemological frame: "What does it mean to be a Mexican? In what regard are Mexicans held? Is the Mexican identity changing in the United States?" Pondering such issues (or, in fact, forming questions to create new knowledge), Richard is seizing a level of power that most never know is worth pursuing. By engaging himself intellectually, Richard will be controlled by racial intrusions less than the average citizen who simply accepts the presented "knowledge" as is.

Concerning the ontological questions, Richard is almost entranced by the notion of existence. Along the way, Richard learns that while it is true that no human being is better than another, it is also true that no human beings are equal. Richard then concludes that every person is unique and as such brings a special purpose to the human community, a purpose that each individual must discover for himself and then pursue without fail. For Richard, this purpose involves bridging his Mexican self with his artistic self, no matter the press of family circumstance or the encroachment of an otherwise insensitive, if not hostile, outside world. Racial integrity is tantamount to individual human advancement.

BIBLIOGRAPHY

Aranda, Jose F. *When We Arrive: A New Literary History of Mexican America*. Tucson: University of Arizona Press, 2003.

Farmworkers official Web site, "History," Carlos Marentes and Cynthia P. Marentes, www.farmworkers.org (accessed December 3, 2003).

Menchaca, Martha. *Recovering History, Constructing Race: The Indian, Black, and White Roots of Mexican Americans*. Austin: University of Texas Press, 2001.

Neate, Wilson. *Tolerating Ambiguity: Ethnicity and Community in Chicano/a Writing*. New York: Peter Lang, 1998.

Robinson, Cecil. *No Short Journeys: The Interplay of Cultures in the History and Literature of the Borderlands*. Tucson: University of Arizona Press, 1992.

Saldivar, Jose David. *Remapping American Cultural Studies.* Berkeley: University of California Press, 1997.

Trevino, Jesus Salvador. *Eyewitness: A Filmmaker's Memoir of the Chicano Movement.* Houston, TX: Arte Publico Press, 2001.

Villarreal, Jose Antonio. *Pocho.* New York: Doubleday, 1959.

5

Sandra Cisneros, *The House on Mango Street* (1984)

PLOT SYNOPSIS

This novel traces the development of Esperanza Cordero, a Mexican American girl growing up in the increasingly Latino section of Chicago. Not a typical novel, *The House on Mango Street* is told in a series of vignettes. The first-person narrator is Esperanza herself; the observations she makes about the various people she encounters in her neighborhood serve to unify the novel. Some characters appear in more than one vignette so that the reader also charts their subtle development in addition to the transformation that Esperanza makes. Every issue that Esperanza presents is subtle and indistinct, including the subject of race. Because she is only a girl struggling to understand the world around her, the issues are not addressed with the kind of clarity one might like. Instead, the atmosphere of the novel is hazy, and it mirrors Esperanza's confusion about life on Mango Street.

The novel opens with Esperanza explaining how her family came to live on Mango Street. For as long as she can remember, the Corderos have wanted to own a house. Before occupying the present dwelling, they have had to move almost every year to escape incompetent landlords or inhuman living conditions. Though the Mango Street house is not exactly what they wanted, it must suffice for what is now a six-member family: Esperanza, her mother and father, her sister Nenny, and her two brothers Carlos and Kiki.

Because she is the older of the two girls, Esperanza is expected to watch over Nenny, and even though she is also older than the boys, they live in their own world, one that they protect from the girls. Nenny is not as bright as Esperanza, and as a consequence Esperanza feels a special need to protect Nenny. While she yearns for girlfriends her own age who can better understand her, Esperanza never neglects Nenny. On an instinctual level, she understands the importance of caring for family. Still, she would like to be as independent as her great-grandmother, the woman for whom she is named. Refusing to marry, the older Esperanza was practically kidnapped by the man who would be her husband. This family legend gives the younger Esperanza a spiritedness that she would like to express. For the moment, however, she is confined to Mango Street and the demands of sisterly care.

The first friend Esperanza makes is Cathy, a girl who has a house full of cats. Unfortunately, the friendship is short-lived because Cathy's family moves within days of the Corderos' arrival. Cathy does, however, divulge to Esperanza some of the secrets of the various residents. From Cathy, Esperanza also experiences a subtle racism which reminds her that, for many in the United States, those like Esperanza are considered different and inferior.

Just as Cathy exits her life, two new friends enter: Lucy and her younger sister Rachel. The two newcomers convince Esperanza to help them purchase a bicycle that they all can then use. Just happy to have other girls with whom to interact, Esperanza agrees. From now on, she and Nenny spend the greater portion of their time in the company of Lucy and Rachel Guerrero. In addition to the two sisters, Esperanza also befriends the boy who moves into the house that Cathy's family leaves. Juan (or Meme) is described as an awkward and probably retarded boy. Nonetheless, Esperanza and the others allow him to play with them. Unfortunately, he breaks both his arms when he wins the Tarzan jumping contest in his back yard. His accident reflects the kinds of losses and disappointments in life that Esperanza comes to understand, if not expect.

Other moments of excitement filter through Esperanza's life. In the basement of Meme's house is an apartment occupied by a large Puerto Rican family. Among those who live there are two cousins of the family, an older boy and an older girl. On one occasion the unnamed male cousin arrives driving a shiny Cadillac. He takes all the children for a ride through the neighborhood when suddenly everyone hears sirens. The cousin orders all the children out, as he tries to flee the police. He is caught, however, when he wrecks the car at the end of the block. Esperanza finds the girl cousin, Marin, intriguing because of her seemingly worldly ways. She smokes, sells Avon, and knows all the secrets about makeup application and about boys and other adult matters. Esperanza admires her independence; Marin is saving her money so that she can return to Puerto Rico and marry her boyfriend. Esperanza knows that Marin yearns for a life beyond Mango Street, and she herself is increasingly interested in a world beyond her present confines.

While Esperanza is allowed to interact with most everyone on the street, there seems to be a tacit understanding among the decent residents that their children should avoid the Vargas clan. Rosa Vargas has a house full of unruly children whom she must try to raise alone. Nenny is particularly instructed to avoid the Vargas family, lest she become just like them. Because the neighbors expect nothing good from these children, they do not bother to intervene when they spy the children misbehaving. If Rosa cannot manage her own brood, no one else will fill the role of disciplinarian. Esperanza explains that no one hardly ever notices the Vargas family. Even on the day when Angel Vargas leaps from the roof and "explodes" to the ground, no one even bothered to look up. This incident simply becomes one more in a series of events that punctuate life on Mango Street.

Esperanza and her cohorts continue to experience all that Mango Street has to offer as they grow up and try to understand the adult world. On one occasion, an unnamed neighbor bestows upon Esperanza, Lucy, and Rachel three pairs of shoes that she is discarding. Happy to have a new distraction, the three girls prance up and down the street in their high-heel women's shoes. Flattered by the attention they are garnering, even though store proprietor Mr. Benny strongly suggests that they remove the shoes, the three girls parade up and down with even more intent. Soon, however, they come upon a bum whose immediate interest in them is mere seduction. Realizing that they have happened upon a potentially dangerous situation, the girls flee. And when they later discover that their shoes have been inadvertently thrown out by Lucy and Rachel's mother, they are not upset. Because they grew up almost a bit too fast, they happily return to the stuff of child's play.

Part of her development involves Esperanza's coming to terms with the fact that some of her desires are misguided; that is, what might seem desirable is proven to be the opposite. Esperanza is enchanted by her classmates who have the "privilege" of staying at school during the lunch hour. Those like her, who live close by, are required to return home for lunch. Esperanza wants desperately to stay at school and eat with the "canteen kids," and she finally convinces her mother to draft a note to school officials asking if she might join this group of students. However, on the one day when she is allowed to remain at school, Esperanza discovers that the lunch she prepared at home is now soggy, greasy, and cold. The other kids look at her like she does not belong; what she had thought would be a time spent in joy and camaraderie is, in fact, a time of disappointment and frustration.

Like all adolescents, Esperanza feels the occasional awkwardness. At the party for her cousin's baptism, Esperanza shies away from attention because she is forced to wear her everyday shoes when her mother forgets to purchase new ones to match Esperanza's new dress and socks. Feeling self-conscious about her appearance, she refuses to dance with boys her age. However, her uncle urges her to dance with him, telling her that she is the most beautiful girl in attendance. Acquiescing, Esperanza finds herself floating on the dance floor with her Uncle Nacho. They are the stars of the dance floor, and Esperanza gains much confidence as a result of her experience. When her mother beams with pride, Esperanza feels a special joy. Uncle Nacho forces her to overcome her fear, and she soars in the process.

After Esperanza enters high school, she decides that she needs a job to help pay for the tuition at the Catholic school. Maturing and wanting to take more responsibility for her life, Esperanza is thrilled when her Aunt Lala secures a job for her at the photo shop where Aunt Lala herself works. Venturing far from Mango Street on a regular basis for the first time, Esperanza is somewhat nervous about interacting with the other workers. She eats alone during break, and she does not engage the others in conversation. Finally an "Oriental" man befriends her (or seems to) and invites her to eat with him from now on. He then informs her that today is his birthday and asks her to give him a kiss to celebrate. As she proceeds to kiss him on the cheek, the old man plants the kiss firmly on her lips and holds on to her interminably. Esperanza learns, of course, that the real world has many dangers lurking about, even in the guise of what seems safe and secure.

Esperanza is made to feel vulnerable as well when death suddenly visits the Corderos. When her father gets word that his own father has died back in Mexico, he is saddened to a degree that Esperanza has never before witnessed. She feels vulnerable when she witnesses her father's grief, and she begins to ponder what it must feel like to lose a father. As the oldest, she is charged with telling the other children, and while this responsibility fortifies her, Esperanza is still left with an empty feeling. On the heels of this loss, her Aunt Lupe, who has long suffered a terminal illness, succumbs. Esperanza feels a special loss here because Lupe always encouraged her to write, while listening attentively as Esperanza recited poems and stories. These losses do compel Esperanza to consider exactly how she wishes to live her life. Before she dies, Lupe stresses to Esperanza that her writing is her freedom and that expression is tantamount to liberation. Esperanza takes her Aunt Lupe's lesson to heart. Concerned now about her future, Esperanza, seeking the advice of a fortune teller (or witch woman), learns only that she will have "a home in the heart." Though she does not fully understand the meaning of these words, she is left with something to consider.

Other unique characters people Mango Street and provide for Esperanza's life texture and substance. Living next door with her mother Edna, who owns a large apartment building, is the childlike, yet fully grown Ruthie. As described by Esperanza, Ruthie is the only adult who likes to play with the children. Still, she is quite shy around other adults. When she accompanies the children to the store, she refuses to enter, instead waiting outside while the children make her purchases. Though Ruthie supposedly has a husband to whom she intends to return, no one has ever seen this husband, and Ruthie continues to live with Edna. Esperanza is also fascinated by Earl, the Tennessee native whose southern accent betrays his roots. A jukebox repairman who favors the children in the neighborhood with records from his vast collection, Earl, supposedly has a wife, though only Esperanza's mother and Edna have ever seen her. While Esperanza thinks she has seen Earl's wife, her description of the woman disputes that of her mother. The woman a naive Esperanza describes, however, is more than likely a prostitute, with her red hair and tight pink pants (her visits to Earl's house are always brief). Across the street from Esperanza is the recently arrived Mamacita, the rather corpulent mother of Esperanza's neighbor who has saved his money for quite a while to bring his mother and a baby boy from Mexico. Mamacita never leaves the apartment, and she has learned only select English phrases. When the baby boy begins to speak and proceeds to learn English commercial jingles, Mamacita is horrified. Determined to preserve her Spanish-speaking heritage, she cautions the baby, "No speak English." Missing her homeland and her native culture, the old woman despairs at the changes she is forced to confront.

While Mamacita has imprisoned herself, another Mango Street inhabitant finds herself locked in her apartment every Tuesday when her husband leaves to play dominoes. Fearing Rafaela might run away because she is so beautiful, the unnamed husband locks her in the apartment. The children have become so accustomed to seeing her sit in the window that they do not notice her until she beckons them and asks if they will trek to the market and buy her papaya and/or coconut juice. These sweet drinks provide her only pleasure in an otherwise lonely existence.

The one character to whom several vignettes are devoted is Esperanza's friend Sally, whose story somewhat centers the latter portion of the novel. Because Sally is very beautiful, her father is extremely protective of her. He even beats her for fear she will succumb to the wiles of the boys who most certainly desire her. Because his sisters fled from home at a young age, he fears that Sally will do the same. The anger he feels for his sisters he lodges at Sally. Matters in her home become so desperate that Sally moves in with Esperanza's family, but only for a few hours. Her father calls for her, and after he apologizes and begs her to return home, Sally leaves with him. Several days later, upon spying Sally talking to a boy, the father proceeds to beat Sally uncontrollably. Ultimately, Sally's only recourse is to marry the first man she finds somewhat appealing. The marshmallow salesman takes her to another state where it is legal to marry a minor. Though she insists she is happy with her new husband, Sally is in reality imprisoned by a man who is just as jealous and overprotective as her father.

All of these characters and a few others impact Esperanza and her outlook for the future. She decides that her Mexican American female self must rise above the circumstances that define life on Mango Street. The novel ends with Esperanza making preliminary decisions about a future grounded in, yet far removed from, that little house on Mango Street.

HISTORICAL BACKGROUND

The House on Mango Street, published in 1984, is set in a rapidly changing Chicago neighborhood, most likely in the 1960s. As more and more Mexicans and other Latinos move into the area, long-term residents (mostly white) leave for the suburbs. The novel addresses a typical sociological phenomenon of the period leading up to its publication date—the 1960s, 1970s, and early 1980s. From the 1960s on, Chicago emerged as one of the most populated Mexican communities in the country, ranking third behind Los Angeles and San Antonio. The reason for this rapid increase is the history of Mexicans in Chicago. As early as the 1910s, more and more immigrants from Mexico came to the United States to flee the Mexican Revolution and its ensuing chaos. In the early twentieth century, Chicago's famed

Southside housed steel mills and many other industries that supported the mills. Mexican men came in droves to accept jobs in this expanding industry. Quickly establishing their own living quarters, these immigrants attracted more Mexicans to the area until the Southside had its own little Mexican colony.

Even though these laborers worked hard to succeed in the U.S. system, they still took pride in their Mexican heritage. Theirs would be a kind of dual identity, both Mexican and American. While the American identity provided the momentum and encouragement for economic and social success, the Mexican identity provided cultural and spiritual harmony. The Mexican past is ever present in the daily mindset of these U.S. citizens, especially in those from the older generation. This kind of duality Esperanza notes several times in the various vignettes. Whether she is discussing Juan (Meme) Ortiz's sheepdog with the two names (one in English and one in Spanish), or whether she is describing the meaning of her own name in Spanish and in English, or whether she is detailing Mamacita's dogged determination to retain her facility with Spanish at the expense of learning English, Esperanza historicizes for the reader the importance of cultural and racial awareness among Chicago's Mexican people.

Such awareness has even been instilled in the younger generation, as is evidenced in Esperanza's need to retain a little bit of Mexico on Mango Street. One day while walking down the street with Nenny and friends Lucy and Rachel, Esperanza sees a house that for some reason reminds her of houses she has seen in Mexico. Even though Rachel and Lucy think she is odd for imposing a Mexican memory onto a decidedly American place, Nenny comes to Esperanza's defense and states that the house looks exactly like Mexico (not a house in Mexico, but Mexico). For the older and younger Corderos, a strong racial identity is very important; they do not apologize for latching on to any symbol or cultural icon that gives them a sense of racial security.

This sense of connectedness to Mexico is somewhat shattered for the Cordero family when they learn that Esperanza's paternal grandfather has died. Never before has Esperanza seen her own father so racked with grief. While she knows he sobs for his lost father, it is also evident that he cries for the loss of connection to his homeland. He also sobs because he had to leave that homeland in order to forge what he considered a better life for his family. As he prepares to go to Mexico to bury his father, Esperanza's father knows on some level that this one journey of reverse migration will mark a final goodbye to all he knew and loved in Mexico. Losing a parent is tantamount to losing a part of oneself in general; when one adds the cultural and racial dimensions to this loss, he or she can feel a special vulnerability. The security of homeland (represented by his father's life) is no longer a function of Esperanza's father's world.

Esperanza's father grieves for the loss and the sacrifice. He remembers the different turns his life has taken since he came to the United States, from the early days when the only English words he knew were "ham-and-eggs" to the present moment when he owns a house. Even though he may be considered inferior by some in the majority, he is still a man who has accomplished a measure of success. In contrast to his story is that of Geraldo, the non-English speaking immigrant killed in a hit-and-run accident, whom Marin met at a club. He is one of many nameless Mexican immigrants who have come to the United States and on to Chicago to work hard and send money back home to family in Mexico. When Geraldo dies, no one knows whom to contact because no one has ever really known him fully. As Esperanza surmises (from the perspective of the majority population), Geraldo was "just another *brazer* who didn't speak English. Just another wetback. You know the kind. The ones who always look ashamed" (Cisneros, *The House on Mango Street*, 66). Geraldo's family back in Mexico will never know what has happened to him; he will simply be among the lost. Though he was an individual with hopes and aspirations (evident in his financial commitment to family back home), Geraldo is dismissed as just another dirty, shameful "wetback." Unlike Esperanza's father who, while not at all wealthy, has enjoyed a modicum of American success, Geraldo is denied the possibility of proving himself further. Because he is Mexican, his American legacy will be a stereotyped American version of a wasted Mexican life.

Geraldo's history and that of Esperanza's father provide a comprehensive view of the Mexican American experience beyond the racist notions often imposed on that experience.

LITERARY ANALYSIS

The dominant theme in the novel is the right to pursue freedom and the right to make choices in life despite one's race or despite the restrictions society attempts to impose on one because of race. The very fact that Esperanza and her family live on Mango Street is proof that they refuse to be defined by the racist intrusions and barriers of the United States. Before coming to Mango Street, the Corderos lived in a series of rental properties, most of which were unfit for human habitation. The squalid conditions in which they found themselves, the landlords obviously thought, were suitable for these "insignificant" Mexicans. However, the Corderos militate against the socioeconomic oppression thrust upon them. Though the United States may think that renting and living in despicable circumstances is fine for them, Esperanza's family believe they are worthy of the life of so-called typical (i.e., white) Americans. The little house on Mango Street represents for them stability and rootedness. For the first time, they own their house, and they are no longer subjected to the whims of unethical landlords who refuse to repair burst water pipes or restore the property to at least a semblance of decency. Race in this novel is inextricably tied to economic mobility. The Corderos refuse to be defined by economic confinement; they insist on the right for mobility and for a decent home for their children.

Still, the house on Mango Street does not fulfill their more vivid dreams. They do fantasize about living in a large house with three bathrooms. Instead, each child must share a bedroom, and they have only one bathroom. Nevertheless, when they occupied their previous dwelling, they had to share facilities with other tenants. While Mango Street might not fulfill all of their dreams of economic freedom and equality with the majority society, it does represent a marked improvement over their previous circumstances, and it marks progress along this road of both economic and ethnic upliftment.

More important is the fact that the Mango Street dwelling affords Esperanza not only a sense of place, but also a sense of worth. Esperanza recalls that once when her family rented an apartment above a boarded-up laundromat, one of her school nuns happened by and asked her if, in fact, she lived there. The tone of the nun's voice made Esperanza feel like she was nothing. By definite contrast, Mango Street makes her feel like something, and although the little house pales in comparison to the one the family has always dreamed of, the modest house represents the Corderos' freedom and, to a great extent, Esperanza's freedom as well.

Mango Street itself provides the nexus for assessing race and bias. As more Mexican Americans move into the neighborhood, the whites flee. Esperanza comes face to face with the white fear of the "browning" of the neighborhood when she tries to befriend one of the remaining white girls on the street. Cathy, whose family's move is imminent, agrees to be Esperanza's friend during her remaining week living there. While Cathy initially seems friendly, it soon becomes apparent that she has been indoctrinated into the subtleties of racism. Without flinching, Cathy, who prides herself on her French heritage, explains to Esperanza that her family must leave Mango Street because the neighborhood is deteriorating, making this comment without any sense that it is offensive to Esperanza who has just moved there. While Cathy might consider herself a friend to Esperanza, an individual, she has already begun to harbor a deep-seated prejudice against the entire Mexican group. Though Esperanza is hurt by Cathy's remarks, she learns a valuable lesson about the intricacies of race relations and how the majority really feels when it believes its "superior" position is threatened.

Esperanza understands that Cathy's "friendship" is not real, and when she is tested about where her loyalties should lie, Esperanza proves her understanding of the importance of racial solidarity when confronted with someone like Cathy. Just a day or two before Cathy is to leave, she and Esperanza happen upon Lucy and Rachel Guerrero, two Mexican American sisters whom Cathy does not like, ostensibly because of their disheveled appearance. Esperanza, on the other hand, is enamored of what she describes as their "crooked and old" clothes. Lucy and Rachel appear to Esperanza as sincere girls who simply want new friends. When she decides to join the two, Cathy disappears. Here, Esperanza makes a strategic choice. On the one hand, since Cathy is leaving the neighborhood anyway, Esperanza is better off befriending girls who will remain on Mango Street. On the other hand, Esperanza is sensitive to being ostracized or being made to feel inferior (recall her encounter with the nun) simply because of one's circumstances. Lucy and Rachel's presence provides Esperanza with a means of tapping into the human dignity that is so inextricably bound to her Mexican sense of identity and security. Like the hair on her head that "never obeys barrettes or bands" (6), Esperanza shuns the kind of confinement represented by Cathy's prejudice. Her liberated hair underscores her increasingly liberated self. After joining up with Lucy and Rachel and purchasing a used bike with them, Esperanza enjoys wheeling up and down Mango Street with the two girls in tow "laughing the crooked ride back" (16). Esperanza has turned what Cathy saw as a negative, the girls' "crooked" appearance, into a positive. All three girls—Lucy, Rachel, and Esperanza—revel in their uniqueness.

The "crookedness" that people like Cathy attempt to objectify Esperanza validates in the subject position. Rather than being objects of derision, Esperanza and her two new friends occupy the majority position, not just on the rapidly transforming Mango Street, but also in their own minds. Esperanza notes in a single vignette that outsiders who come into her neighborhood are scared when they quickly find themselves in the minority. She insists, however, that there is nothing to fear there. All of the strange residents she knows, and she is comfortable with them. Though an outsider may think of them as dangerous, Esperanza does not think of them as so. These outsiders she considers to be both "stupid" and "lost." The "brown" people on Mango Street, implies Esperanza, are not dangerous simply because they are brown. For Esperanza, in fact, the following is true: "All brown all around, we are safe" (28). This "brown" neighborhood is a haven, a place where one feels secure. Establishing herself and those like her in the subject position (and not as objects or pariahs), Esperanza refutes the widely held notion that this Mexican neighborhood harbors only the inhuman and the vile. Esperanza insists that her neighbors instill fear in outsiders only because they are different and not because of some inherent evil in them. From her majority perspective, Esperanza even notes that when someone like her goes into a different ethnic neighborhood, she, too, is frightened. Esperanza explores the notion of racial difference in this observation. She subverts the idea that one should fear Mexicans for being Mexican. Instead, she suggests that one might fear Mexicans because they are different from the outsider who is observing. Racism stems from a fear of difference more so than it does from actual knowledge of the inhumanity of a given group. To suggest that non-Mexicans might cause her to be frightened shatters the notion of (white) superiority over the Mexican presence.

Every time Esperanza uses her intellectual gifts, she fights against racism and racial confinement. As Esperanza's dying aunt states to her, writing "will keep you free" (61). When Esperanza gives written form to her observations about the world around her and when she analyzes the social order, she is better able to distinguish between society's arbitrary dictates and higher laws of ethics and morality with regard to human interaction. Writing frees her from the kind of indoctrination that would have her believe she is inferior. Because she has begun her "own quiet war" (89), Esperanza will not be controlled by the bloated might of others. When Esperanza learns that her mother, once a bright student herself, left school only because she was ashamed of her ragged clothes, she knows that she cannot succumb to the same kind of shame. Her mother's economic condition, which also dominated her racial identity, caused the kind of pain and intellectual sacrifice that Esperanza wishes to spare herself. To showcase

her academic skill and to militate against all forces that would undermine her gifts is tantamount to projecting pride in her Mexican self.
The shame that her mother felt is the same shame that Cathy tries to
foist upon Lucy and Rachel, in an attempt to make them feel inferior.
When her mother teaches, "Shame is a bad thing, you know. It keeps
you down" (91), Esperanza understands that she owes it to her
mother, her entire family and community even, to exploit her talents
and to succeed no matter what. Given her mother's frustrated past
and given her knowledge of the Cathys of the world, Esperanza knows
that in order to be the best Mexican American woman she can be, she
must develop her natural talents to their fullest extent. For her, the
freedom to rise above racial and racist intrusions is bound both to the
pride she has for Mango Street and to the commitment she has to self,
beyond the confines of this same street.

BIBLIOGRAPHY

Chicago Historical Society, "History," www.chicagohs.org (accessed January
    3, 2004).
Chicago's Mexican Community Web site, "Historiography," Ray Hutchin-
    son, www.aztlan.net/chicagoh.htm (accessed January 3, 2004).
Cisneros, Sandra. *The House on Mango Street.* New York: Vintage, 1991;
    originally published in 1984.
Cruz, Felicia J. "On the 'Simplicity' of Sandra Cisneros's *The House on
    Mango Street.*" *Modern Fiction Studies* 47, no. 4 (2001): 910–46.
Olivares, Julian. "Entering *The House on Mango Street.*" In *Teaching Ameri-
    can Ethnic Literatures: Nineteen Essays,* edited by John R. Maitino and
    David R. Peck, 209–35. Albuquerque: University of New Mexico
    Press, 1996.
Salazer, Ines. "Can You Go Home Again? Transgression and Transformation
    in African-American Women's and Chicana Literary Practice." In *Post-
    colonial Theory and the United States: Race, Ethnicity, and Literature,*
    edited by Amritjit Singh and Peter Schmidt, 388–411. Jackson: Uni-
    versity Press of Mississippi, 2000.
Sloboda, Nicholas. "A Home in the Heart: Sandra Cisnero's *The House on
    Mango Street.*" *Aztlan: A Journal of Chicano Studies* 22, no. 2 (1997):
    89–106.

6

Margaret Craven, *I Heard the Owl Call My Name* (1973)

PLOT SYNOPSIS

Unaware that he has less than three years to live, Mark Brian, a young vicar, is sent from Vancouver, British Columbia, to the Pacific Northwest to serve as spiritual leader of an isolated Native American village. When his bishop learns of the vicar's illness, the elder bishop decides to send his young charge to the village to learn from the Native Americans and to learn about what is important in life (and in death).

The novel opens with Mark making the two-day boat trip to the village of Kingcome with his assigned Native American guide Jim. As they remove farther and farther from civilization, Mark begins to realize just how different his life will be. As they meander along the sea and various islands, Mark tries to recall as much as he can about his new congregants from his conversations with the bishop. Upon arriving, Mark finds the people there are more reserved than Jim, and they eye Mark with some suspicion. Because they have had little contact with whites, the Native Americans must first observe Mark's demeanor before they display any outward signs of acceptance. The bishop has warned Mark that he must employ patience in interacting with the locals, advice which Mark takes seriously.

Mark's first major task is to attend to the burial of a recently drowned boy. The body of the youngster has been kept in the vicarage for 10 days because no official from the Indian Affairs Department has come to issue the requisite burial permit. Mark gets a quick lesson in how some from the outside world regard the Native Americans. That a dead body is delayed burial for such a long time is offensive to Mark, and such treatment is made even more offensive when the official finally arrives and begins to berate the locals. Constable Pearson criticizes the Native Americans for having removed the body from the scene of the death, even though the body would have washed away had the community allowed it to remain near the water. After wielding his authority, Pearson releases the permit and abruptly leaves. Mark honors the request of the locals and officiates at the open-air ceremony. He does not intrude any more than is necessary, in an attempt to offer the least possible offense. When he completes his part of the ceremony, he excuses himself. On leaving, he notices that the Native Americans remain and conclude the burial ritual by chanting in their native tongue.

Over the next several hours, the villagers gather in small groups to discuss the new vicar. They comment on his manners, his apparent respect for their customs, and even the cleanliness of his fingernails. Key leaders in the community, both male and female, wonder to what extent Mark will be sincerely concerned for them and, as a result, how quickly he will strive to learn of their most pressing needs. Mrs. Hudson, matriarch of the one of the best houses in the village, wonders if the bishop will visit more frequently now that a new vicar has been installed. She looks forward to hosting the bishop and other dignitaries whom he might bring. Marta Stephens, one of the grandmothers, will also vie for the bishop's attention; she also anticipates more social activity. T. P. Wallace, one of the elders, wonders how Mark will respond to the transformations of the younger generation, who no longer appreciate or fully understand the traditional ways. Sam, called the unlucky one (who also abuses his wife and daughter Ellie), wonders if he will have an opportunity to beg the vicar for money before the vicar is warned by the bishop about Sam's unseemly ways. Keetah, Mrs. Hudson's granddaughter, wonders how long it will take Mark to learn that her boyfriend Gordon is restless about his life in Kingcome. All of the villagers, with the exception of Sam, decide to wait, to listen, and to observe their new neighbor.

Over the next few days Mark makes repairs around the church and vicarage, visits the sick, and prepares his first sermon. As the villagers pass by, most of them simply observe Mark in his manual work; a few make comments. Mark senses that they are very slowly warming to him. On the first Sunday, everyone except Sam (whom Mark has refused money), the sick, and the local teacher (who disdains religion) comes to church. Marta even brings him a cap that she has knitted. Even though Mark still feels quite lonely in his new surroundings, he is making a concerted effort to learn about the people and their language. He begins to greet them in Kwakwala, and he notices that they are mildly pleased.

As the fall season progresses and as the days of fishing decrease, more of the Native American men remain in the village. Mark notices that they now take up hunting, and after making inquiry with Jim, he decides to accompany a group on an expedition. However, soon into the venture, Mark realizes that he is not mentally, physically, or spiritually equipped to hunt (or to fish even). He knows now that he must impact the lives of the villagers in other ways.

During the busy Christmas season, Mark and Jim deliver toys sent from churches in Vancouver not only to the village children, but also to those in logging camps and on isolated float houses that are a part of Mark's circuit. Mark observes how dedicated and loyal the entire community is, and he feels he is beginning to understand the struggles they have endured in the recent past and in the distant past. As members of the tribe march single file down for Christmas Eve midnight service, Mark even thinks, "How many times had they traveled thus through the mountain passes down from the Bering Sea?" (Craven, *I Heard the Owl Call My Name*, 58). Considering them comprehensively in this way, Mark "[for] the first time...knew them for what they were, the people of his hand and the sheep of his pasture, and he knew how deep was his commitment to them" (58). In greeting each congregant by name, Mark feels as though he has made a heartfelt connection, and he is pleased that he finally feels a sense of belonging.

Just after the Christmas season and before the older children leave home to return to the English schools, Mark detects tension among the villagers. Upon asking one of the elders, Mark learns that every time the children return from school, they cause a sense of unease among the regular inhabitants. From the English schools they bring a new language, a new culture, and what appears as increased disdain for Native American ways. The children admonish their parents to speak and to behave like whites do. The elders bemoan the fact that their children are changing and that the old ways are being eroded. Though Mark is sensitive to the frustrations of the elders, he knows as well that one day Kingcome will be no more.

Before the school children leave, Mark is befriended by an older boy who is interested in books and intellectual achievement. Gordon, who is being raised by his devoted uncle, is very proud of the giant mask (a family heirloom) that his uncle owns. Gordon shares with Mark the fact that he and his uncle would never part with the mask, even though they have been offered as much as $3,000. Mark senses in Gordon not only Native American pride, but also a deep apprecia- tion for the education he is receiving at the English school; he yearns for more exposure to the outside world. Mark knows already that Gordon will never return to Kingcome permanently; he will be one of many in the next generation to leave behind the world he once knew.

After the children return to the government school, Mark is called to attend to Mrs. Hudson, who has taken ill. Upon arriving, Mark learns that Keetah's sister, Mrs. Hudson's other granddaughter, has written that she will soon marry a white man. Mrs. Hudson fears the changes that such a union will bring, and even though Keetah tries to convince her grandmother that the sister would never abandon her family, Mrs. Hudson cannot seem to shake her fears. Several days later, while Mark is away attending to duties at a nearby village, the sister and her fiancé visit Kingcome. While there the fiancé plies the men with liquor and somehow manipulates Gordon's uncle into selling him the mask for $50. Upon discovery, Keetah's entire family is shamed. Though no one believes that the sister was involved in the transaction, the family still punish themselves by gathering their belongings and re- moving to an isolated and abandoned village. Mark is horrified to wit- ness so many negative changes being visited upon Kingcome.

Three months later Mark learns that Keetah's sister was abandoned in Vancouver by her "fiancé" when she objected to his "stealing" of the mask. She ended up selling herself on the streets and then ulti- mately succumbing to a drug overdose. She died feeling much guilt for her involvement, albeit unknowing involvement, in the incident which brought shame to her family. When Mark is told of the sister's fate, he is plunged into a deep sadness for the community he has begun to understand.

In the late spring, Gordon's mother dies in childbirth. On her deathbed, she pleads with Mark to ensure that Gordon gets an edu- cation, no matter what. Mark, later informing Gordon of his mother's wishes, tells Gordon that he need not worry about his younger sib- lings and that the village will make plans for their care. After the fu- neral, Mark is told that the men in the village are now prepared to help him construct a new vicarage whenever he is ready. Now that Mark has suffered almost a full year along with the Native Americans, they feel as though he is one of them (or as much a part of them as any white man could be), and they gladly offer their assistance.

The materials for the vicarage are delivered in the summer, and for the next six weeks, Kingcome is abuzz with activity. The men work furiously to complete the project before the August rains and before another first-time event: the Native Americans will be allowed to purchase liquor. After the building is completed, the bishop and some accompanying clergy pay a visit to bless the structure and to enjoy a grand feast. While Mark is pleased with this accomplishment, still another matter causes him much concern. The men become increasingly dissipated. By mid-August, they spend in excess of $2,000 on liquor, and by month's end, they have spent $6,000.

Taking a much needed break, in September Mark joins Jim in escorting four boys, including Gordon, to Vancouver where they will continue their education. While back home, Mark visits his twin sister, his only living relative. He also visits with some old school chums and an old professor. Mark feels so detached from these people, however. Their concerns, even the words they speak, are no longer his. Mark is happy to return to Kingcome, and he is even more pleased when he discovers that much of the dissipation has ceased. It seems that con artist Sam is to thank for the change. When an intoxicated Sam loses a recently purchased washing machine when it falls overboard his boat, his wife beats him mercilessly, locks him out of the house, and will not allow him to enter until he agrees to send their daughter Ellie to school. Sam's indiscretion has a "sobering" effect on the other men, too.

The second fall of Mark's assignment passes without incident, and Christmas quickly approaches. Mark is pleased when a very mature and poised Gordon returns for the holiday. The older villagers are concerned that Gordon now cuts his hair and speaks quite differently. They want Mark to convince Gordon that he must return home and assume a leadership position in his community. Mark, however, will not intervene, insisting that Gordon's life should be in Gordon's control. Gordon decides he must leave forever, and he takes Keetah with him.

However, in March Keetah returns, having found the outside world unappealing. For two weeks, she avoids contact with Mark. When she finally comes to him, she reveals that she stayed with Gordon only long enough to become pregnant with his child. Though Mark does not and will never understand her motives, she states very simply that she felt a responsibility to bring back to Kingcome a part of Gordon, the man who she feels must somehow be a part of his homeland. Jim, who has always wanted to marry Keetah, agrees to marry her now and make her child his own.

In late spring, Mark, finally taking a good look at himself, realizes that he is wasting away and that he is to die soon. While he is making preparations to return to Vancouver, Keetah approaches him, as spokesperson for the tribe, and asks that he remain with them until the end. Touched by this gesture, Mark realizes that his real home is now here in Kingcome. Later on the same day, Mark and Jim are summoned to go in search of a logger who is lost at sea. After venturing out, they learn by radiophone that the logger, a drunkard who stole the boat he fled in, is safe. As they prepare to return to Kingcome Inlet, they are caught in a violent storm, in the midst of which Mark dies. The novel ends with Mark's Native American family preparing his remains for burial in Kingcome. It is clear that Mark (whose spirit the Native Americans believe will return to them) and the villagers of Kingcome are forever changed.

HISTORICAL BACKGROUND

I Heard the Owl Call My Name, published in 1973, is set in the latter 1960s in the Pacific Northwest of British Columbia. The novel, in addition to chronicling Mark Brian's sojourn with the native people of Kingcome village, also provides a glimpse into the lives of the Tsawataineuk tribe who inhabit Kingcome. They are part of the Kwakiutl band of Native Americans who thrive in the broader vicinity. This particular tribe was allotted Kingcome as a reserve in 1886.

While pinpointing the exact time of their arrival is hard, earliest documents suggest that the Kwakiutl began to settle in the region about 10,000 years ago. For the most part, they settled along the coastline in order to exploit the fishing opportunities that the plentiful salmon supply allowed. As time progressed, they also ventured inland to hunt wild game, including deer, bear, elk, and the like.

Northwest Coast Native Americans maintained a very rigid social system, structured along class lines determined by wealth and family influence. Three main classes comprised the social group: nobles, common people, and slaves. The latter occupied that position as a result of war captivity, indebtedness, or parental link to slavery. For the upper class, one's wealth was important as a signal of what one could offer during the important potlatch ceremonies. Such an event was held to dedicate a new building, celebrate a wedding, or acknowledge a rite of passage. Great feasts were held with storytelling, singing, drumming, and speechmaking. Those who could afford the sacrifice would give away, or "share," some of their property, like furs and blankets.

Families were highly respectful of each other, and children were especially respectful of their elders. The chief of a given clan, or group, was honored with the highest regard.

When Mark arrives in Kingcome, he realizes almost immediately that his soon-to-be neighbors are in no way barbaric or simplistic. Though, in comparison to the life he knew back in Vancouver, the Native Americans lead simple lives, they are as complex as the whites he has known. Their racial and cultural difference in no way makes them inferior to him. Because they have had relatively little sustained contact with whites, the Tsawataineuk have retained the overall integrity of their culture. Their long history in Kingcome has afforded them the kind of primacy that does not easily relinquish its cultural value, even in the face of so-called "superior" beings.

The emotional and spiritual strength of the Native Americans results from their embrace of myth. This history of their people is preserved in the myths that are passed down through the generations. These myths, which showcase the fortitude and resilience of the Native Americans, constitute the reality upon which they continue to thrive. No matter what the white man's opinion of them and no matter what his attempt to corral and restrict them in the physical world, the Native Americans protect their present with the elusive (not to be appropriated by outsiders) construct of myth. As the bishop relates to Mark, before he arrives in Kingcome, "The Indian knows his village and feels for his village as no white man for his country.... His village is not the strip of land four miles long and three miles wide.... The myths are the village ...(19). According to Tsawataineuk myth, two brothers, the only persons in the world to survive the great flood, were spiritually moved to come to the area which they called Quee (or "inside place") and would later be known as Kingcome. For the present-day Native Americans, Kingcome is an enchanted place that no interlopers, white or otherwise, can diminish. History and myth, at least for the elders, combine to ward off racial imposition from the white world.

Mark comes to Kingcome at a crucial turning point in the lives of the Tsawataineuk and whites. The younger generation has begun to leave the immediate area and attend school in nearby Alert Bay, and while Mark is there, they have begun to leave and travel all the way to Vancouver. In addition, the Native Americans who choose to remain in their homeland are allowed to purchase alcohol legally. All of these circumstances, for differing reasons, will undermine Native American culture and racial solidarity. The elders are looking back to their ancestors and to their history for guidance, while the young like Gordon and the other boys are looking to the future, and for them, the future means further assimilation into the white man's world.

LITERARY ANALYSIS

In *I Heard the Owl Call My Name,* the issue of race is presented via the theme of natural law versus civil law. The Native American villagers embrace natural law, while the white society is governed by civil law (or the law of civilization, known historically as man-made law). Natural law, however, is defined as the higher law (sometimes referred to as God's law), which determines that human beings are granted the right to thrive (to feed, shelter, clothe, and reproduce themselves) simply by virtue of existing. Natural law, in essence, liberates, while civil law restricts and orders. The written civil law is ostensibly established to maintain order in a "civilized" society. However, in this novel, the theoretical and actual definitions of civil law come into conflict.

Very early on, Mark understands that the Kingcome villagers enjoy a symbiotic relationship with their environment. These "natural" people are, in fact, one with nature. They do not consider themselves separate from the physical world created by the Supreme Being. For Mark, "the Indians belonged here as the birds and fish belonged, ...they were as much a part of the land as the mountains themselves" (37). The village, Mark comes to know, is the river, the salmon, and the grizzly; and the myths also define the village. For the Native Americans, their success is determined by how they learn to live harmoniously with nature, how they learn to cooperate and survive on a daily basis. There is no separation of their spiritual selves and their physical selves and space. Their focus is on community and mutual respect. Ironically, their natural space is more civil than the "civilized" world governed by intellect-infused human law.

This civil world, represented by Mark and the other whites who visit Kingcome, is marred by materialism, competition, and unethical behavior. Though Mark does not behave like the typical whites who come to visit, the villagers force him to prove himself and his humanity during his first months in Kingcome. They monitor and observe him to see if he will interact with them in a condescending and haughty manner. They want to know if he will expect them to be his servants or if he will work as hard as they do. In this "natural" world, everyone is expected to contribute to the greater good of the community. While a certain authority is bestowed upon Mark because of his status as vicar, he is still not supposed to lord said status over his congregants.

The other whites who come to Kingcome bring with them attitudes of superiority and detachment. When Mark arrives, one of the first persons he meets is the teacher, who is in his second year on the island. Mark quickly learns that the teacher hates the Native Americans and that they hate him. The unnamed teacher has come to Kingcome only for the extra pay he will receive for agreeing to teach in a remote location. He intends on using the money to travel to Greece "[to study] the civilization he adored" (33). The teacher has no desire to learn anything from his stay among the Native Americans. In his estimation, they are an inferior people who merit no true respect. After all, Greek (i.e., European; white) "civilization" is more worthy of attention. Though he has come to Kingcome from the so-called civilized world, the teacher is rather barbaric in his attitude, speaking to the Native Americans with disdain and a complete disregard for their humanity. In this community of nonwhites, his whiteness has made him a kind of pariah whom the Native Americans all but ignore. They do not consider him a teacher because he can impart no knowledge to them that will impact their lives in Kingcome. As Mark has known from the beginning of his stay, the Native Americans are the real teachers, and people like him should learn as much as possible from them.

Perhaps the most offensive visitors from the "civilized" world are a group of affluent U.S. citizens who arrive suddenly one day by yacht. The four men and three women objectify the Kingcome village, treating it as though it is an exotic outpost rather than as a place where people conduct their lives in a manner respectful of the customs and traditions they have honored for centuries. Their shrill voices and disrespectful comments about the totems and the Native Americans themselves perturb Mark, who still, however, remains civil to them. Theirs is an overt prejudice: they wonder why a white man like Mark would live there, and they wonder how Mark can tell the Native Americans apart from each other. Never offering any rude responses to them, Mark does, however, decline from taking them back to their yacht in his speed boat, informing them that they must return to their vehicle in the same logger's boat that they took to come ashore. When they depart, Mark is happy to watch them return to a world he no longer knows. Their very uncivil behavior has confirmed for him that the world he now inhabits is far superior to the life and the people he once embraced. These loud Americans represent the worst of conspicuous consumption and inhumanity.

Without question the most "dangerous" white to arrive is an English anthropologist, "a large mannish, gray-haired woman" (102) who is arrogant in what she believes to be her vast knowledge of the Native Americans. Deluding herself that she knows what is best for these "primitive" people, she bemoans the fact that white people ever intruded on these innocents. What would seem to be her liberal and protective stance is made problematic because she is possessed of no self-analysis. She thinks she is right simply because she has studied and intellectualized about the Native Americans. Yet she never critiques herself or her agenda. Her lack of understanding is dangerous because she thinks she understands fully. She refers to this tribe as the Quackadoodles, and even when Mark informs her that they refer to themselves as the Kwakiutls, she snaps back that in England they have been called the Quackadoodles for the past century and that they will continue to be called such. Clearly, in refusing to allow the Native Americans self-definition, the anthropologist objectifies and belittles them. Yet she does not have the presence of mind to realize the potential harm of her attitude. Like the offensive Americans and the teacher, this "civilized" woman of science is presented as inhumane and boorish.

As Mark spends more time with the villagers (and as he continues to observe the ill-informed attitudes of the whites), he realizes that the Native Americans are not to be easily defined by outsiders; they are not to be pigeonholed. Writing to the bishop during his first few months in Kingcome, Mark reveals, "I have learned little of the Indians as yet. I know only what they are not. They are none of the things one has been led to believe. They are not simple, or emotional, they are not primitive" (55–56). What Mark has come to realize is that these nonwhite people are far more advanced in their sense of purpose and in their spiritual presence than are those like him who hail from the "civilized" world from which Mark is becoming ever more detached.

The Native Americans simply do not see themselves as the "other," even if whites do define them as such. They have a keen awareness and respect for their cultural rootedness, one marked not by inferiority but defined by the standard to uphold. They judge life and existence by standards they have set; their reality (or worldview) is to be respected and protected. Such confidence allows them to see the chinks in the white man's cultural armor, and in very subtle ways, they make him pay for his cultural arrogance. Toying with the white man in this way confirms their sense of cultural normalcy. For example, the women in the village undermine the bishop's "superiority" by serving him mashed turnips, when they know, as indicated in Mrs. Hudson's thoughts, that the white man hates mashed turnips. In this and in other ways, they militate against white authority and combat racial intrusion. Because they are comfortable in their own skin, they are not so easily influenced by the cultural imposition of others. When Mrs. Hudson takes ill upon discovering that her granddaughter intends to marry a white man, others assume that she fears her granddaughter will become ashamed of her Native American family. However, Mrs. Hudson quickly informs them: "What I fear is that we will be ashamed of her" (65). In this simple comment, Mrs. Hudson retains Native American authority over the situation and dismisses whatever cultural authority whites may think they have. Mrs. Hudson does not care if her granddaughter, now a part of the white world, is ashamed of her. Later, when the village discovers that the granddaughter's "fiancé" has stolen away with Gordon's family mask, Mrs. Hudson blames the white world's intrusion on Kingcome for the offense. In short, for the elders of Kingcome like Mrs. Hudson, the white world is linked to all that is troubling in mankind.

The Native Americans who are not duped by cultural intrusions have retained control of their own minds, never accepting what is presented to them as the only knowledge. Mark soon learns that the elder villagers in particular never accept the beliefs of outsiders and that they are always braced to offer an opposing (and generally more insightful) view. Even the bishop understands this uncanny ability to a great degree. He shares with Mark the story of Tagoona, an Eskimo priest who, when first ordained, was informed by one white authority figure that he could now help his people with their problems. Not understanding the notion of "a problem," Tagoona is told by the white man that if the white man held him aloft by his feet and threatened to drop him that he (Tagoona) would have a problem. Tagoona, after pondering this predicament, responds by saying that if the white man released him, all would be well, but if the white man chose to drop him, nothing would matter to Tagoona and the white man would have the problem.

This kernel of wisdom exemplifies the kind of intellectual and emotional sophistication nurtured in the natural world of the Native Americans. While race prejudice would define the Kingcome village and other native villages as inferior, *I Heard the Owl Call My Name* underscores the fact that cultural solvency is determined not by outsiders but instead by those who are truly vested in the cultural space being observed. Mark Brian comes as close as any outsider can to understanding the lives of the Kwakiutls, and even he is aware of the fact that he, like any other white man, will never know them fully (137). His awareness of this truth (his lack of arrogance), however, offers the chance of racial understanding, greater than what has previously been possible.

BIBLIOGRAPHY

British Columbia First Nation Web site, "Culture," www.bcfn.org (accessed February 4, 2004).

Craven, Margaret. *I Heard the Owl Call My Name.* New York: Dell, 1973.

Fisher, Robin. *Contact and Conflict: Indian-European Relations in British Columbia, 1774–1890.* Vancouver: University of British Columbia Press, 1992.

Miller, J.R. *Skyscrapers Hide the Heavens: A History of Indian-White Relations in Canada.* Toronto, ON: University of Toronto Press, 1991.

Tennant, Paul. *Aboriginal Peoples and Politics: The Indian Land Question in British Columbia, 1849–1989.* Vancouver: University of British Columbia Press, 1990.

Wallas, Whitaker. *Kwakiutl Legends.* Surrey, BC: Hancock House Publishers, 1982.

7

Leslie Marmon Silko, *Ceremony* (1977)

PLOT SYNOPSIS

Ceremony tells the story of Native American World War II veteran Tayo, a 20-something member of the Laguna tribe who finds himself on a journey toward spiritual recovery. The horrors of war, both captivity and violence, have rendered Tayo emotionally and mentally bankrupt. He spends his days wandering in and out of daydreams, not only about his time in the Philippine jungles, but also about his childhood and the intervening years.

Tayo's life has been fraught with pain and embarrassment almost from its inception. The product of an illicit liaison between a Native American mother and a white man, Tayo has shouldered the stigma of his heritage since age four. When his mother could no longer care for him, she brought him to her older sister Thelma (whom Tayo will forever refer to as Auntie). Along with Auntie, her husband Robert, her son Rocky, her brother Josiah (Tayo's uncle), and her mother (Tayo's Grandma), Tayo lives in a house where he is fortunate to be with family but where he is also subjected to somewhat harsh treatment from Auntie. Tayo is made to feel that his presence brings shame on the family: he is both "illegitimate" and "mixed."

Tayo spends the greater part of his childhood trying to fit into the family. Everyone except Auntie is kind to him. Whenever he is alone with her, she conveys to him her disappointment and frustration with his very existence. Her own son Rocky, she adores, while Tayo she only endures. Auntie has high hopes for Rocky, wanting him to survive off the reservation and make a success of himself. When Rocky (along with Tayo) decides to join the army, Auntie is horrified, but Tayo, who even in his teens is trying to gain full acceptance into the family, promises to return Rocky to the family safely. Though joining an active military is fraught with danger, Tayo believes that he can prove his worthiness both to his family and his country. For the first time, Tayo feels a semblance of brotherhood with Rocky; they become equals in a sense when they both enlist.

Unfortunately, Rocky is killed in battle, and Tayo returns home after the war a broken man, guilt-ridden for having "lost" his cousin and for disappointing Auntie yet again. Tayo knows that Auntie would have preferred that he die in battle and that her son return to her in heroic grandeur. Tayo's position in Auntie's family is even more unstable because he is a daily reminder to her of all that she has lost: her only child and the respectability she has struggled so long to gain in the face of an illegitimate and not-fully-Native American nephew. In short, Tayo now has burdens greater than the ones he had prior to going to war.

In his present mental state, Tayo is haunted by the images he witnessed in battle and by dreams conjured up in his imagination. For him, the present merges with the past and with the future. Upon returning to New Mexico from the Veterans' Hospital where he is recuperating after being rescued, Tayo struggles to gain a sense of reality. When he arrives at the train depot, he is overcome with nausea and physical weakness. When he spies a Japanese family on the street, he collapses. In this one (mentally confusing) moment, Tayo has linked this family with the enemy he fought in battle. His traumatized state compels him to confuse not only the past and the present, but also allies and adversaries.

When the novel opens, Tayo is awakening from a restless night: memories of Rocky, of the now deceased Uncle Josiah, and of the warfare experiences plague him. He is spending time alone at the family's far removed ranch so that he will not fall prey to the drunken exploits of some of the other Native American veterans who seek solace in alcohol and needless violence. Tayo has been left there without transportation and without alcohol. The family hopes that a peaceful isolation will expedite Tayo's recovery. On this particular day, however, Tayo receives a visit from his friend Harley, who arrives on a barely mobile burro. Harley convinces Tayo to join him in search of cold beer and whatever adventure may await them. With Harley on his donkey and Tayo on an old mule, the two make their way to a nearby tavern. Along the way, Tayo confronts various memories, suffers bouts of nausea and confusion, and ultimately collapses.

Undaunted, however, Tayo proceeds with Harley. After having a few beers, Tayo leaves Harley in the bar drinking and talking to himself. Finding a café nearby, Tayo orders some food and reminisces more about the past. He goes back in search of Harley, who has already left. Tayo just continues to walk and walk into the night, visiting places he once frequented with Uncle Josiah and Rocky. He completes this trek by climbing into the barn behind Harley's grandfather's house and falling asleep on a bed of hay. For the first time in a long time, he sleeps all night without (tortured) dreams.

When Tayo next encounters Robert back at the ranch, Robert informs him that Grandma has suggested that Tayo seek the help of a Native American medicine man to restore him to full mental health. Some of the old men in the community also believe that Tayo needs to seek immediate help. Robert then accompanies Tayo into the foothills where he is to meet Betonie, the healer recommended to Grandma. When Robert leaves him with Betonie, Tayo is skeptical at first, feeling quite strongly that the family really want only to remove him so that he will not be a constant embarrassment. Ultimately, though, Tayo warms to Betonie when he realizes that whatever the family's motivation might be that Betonie wishes only to help Tayo.

With Betonie, Tayo travels farther into the mountains, all the while recounting for the old man his experiences in war, as well as his experiences growing up as a pariah. From these stories, Betonie discovers Tayo's "place" in the broader scheme of human existence. From this knowledge, he urges Tayo to see himself as an important product of the human pattern. Betonie is tasked with elevating Tayo beyond the mundane social order to a more harmonious communion with the natural/spiritual world. Betonie reminds Tayo that his Native American heritage (with its stories, rituals, and practices) is a necessary feature in his "restoration." Rather than being defeated by the negative stories of others, Tayo is reminded that he has his own story of empowerment which should serve as his guide in countering the oppressive attempts of antagonistic forces, whether those forces are the jungles of the Pacific, Auntie's hate-filled comments, or his own feelings of insecurity. The storytelling that Betonie engages in becomes itself an important ceremony for Tayo. In this ceremony, Tayo is brought to a more peaceful existence; moreover, he realizes his purpose. He must set out to find and reclaim the spotted cattle lost to his Uncle Josiah while Tayo and Rocky were away at war.

After Tayo leaves Betonie, two events occur that motivate him even more to succeed in finding the cattle and stabilizing himself. First, he is seduced into joining Harley, Leroy (another friend), and a woman (Helen Jean, whom they have recently picked up) on a drinking spree. Luckily, this time, however, Tayo has been strengthened by the interaction with Betonie, and as a result, he sees this experience with renewed clarity. Though he does drink with them, he gains the willpower to make this his last moment of debauchery with these so-called friends. Just before departing from them, Tayo "vomited out everything he had drunk with them, and when that was gone, he was still kneeling on the road beside the truck, holding his heaving belly, trying to vomit out everything—all the past, all his life" (Silko, *Ceremony*, 168). Tayo experiences a catharsis wherein he lays to rest past hurts, frustrations, and disappointments. His focus is now on a future (finding the cattle) that will re-create that past and make Tayo's full life meaningful and relevant.

The second event occurs while he is in pursuit of the cattle after having spied them on the property of a white landowner. Tayo is accosted by two men, described as the cowboy and the Texan, who question him about why he is trespassing. In the meantime, Tayo, of course, loses the cattle once again. The men hold him "hostage," trying to decide what to do with him, when one of them discovers the tracks of a mountain lion. Deciding at this time that catching a mountain lion is more important than catching an Indian, they ultimately release Tayo. Given another chance to prove himself to Betonie and to his family, Tayo redoubles his efforts to locate the cattle and return them to the family ranch. Overnight, a powerful snowstorm pummels the area, a natural occurrence that actually helps Tayo. The rapidly accumulating snow hides Tayo's footprints and the tracks of the cattle. Fearful that the men (and others they may bring with them) will decide later to come in search of him and the livestock, Tayo relaxes somewhat with the advent of the snow.

Before Tayo left Betonie, the old man told him that on his journey, he would see the spotted cattle, a certain configuration of stars, a mountain, and also a woman. Thus far, he has seen all four (the woman he encountered early on his journey). Making his way along in the snow, embracing the kind of weather that might discourage others, Tayo finds himself back at the house of the unnamed woman he had encountered days earlier. To his amazement, the cattle have migrated to her land, and she has succeeded in corralling them. Soon thereafter Tayo returns the livestock to a very happy Robert.

Following his journey, Tayo seems more at ease. Grandma and Robert are particularly pleased with his progress. Auntie, on the other hand, waits for him to resume his bizarre behavior. Forever the pessimist, especially regarding Tayo, Auntie looks for any excuse to belittle him. When Tayo announces at the main house that he intends on returning to the ranch to stay alone, Auntie quickly responds by admonishing him not to welcome any of his drunken "friends" there. Now, fairly unfazed by Auntie and her eruptions, Tayo is concerned only with finding a more harmonious environment that will not disturb the peace of mind he wishes to maintain. At the ranch, he feels close to Rocky and Uncle Josiah, the two people who were always kind to him and whose memories he now takes pride in having honored by restoring the cattle.

After he has been at the ranch for a while, Robert pays a visit to Tayo and informs him that the people back home are worried about him. Emo, another veteran and Tayo's nemesis, has spread rumors that Tayo is crazy again; Robert and the family believe that if Tayo does not return home and prove Emo wrong, the authorities may come and hospitalize Tayo again. Though sensitive to Robert's fears, Tayo decides to stay put. He has found joy not only in his life at the ranch, but also in the love of the woman, now known as Ts'eh, who saved the cattle; unbeknown to everyone else, she (more like a spirit than a person) has joined Tayo at the ranch. An important component in Tayo's "story," she is tasked with helping him where Betonie left off. She reminds him that he is empowered enough to best Emo and his efforts to destroy Tayo. Though confronting his enemies will not be easy, as such a task never is, Tayo can meet the challenge when he understands that he has the power to "write" his story however he chooses, depending of course, as she insists, on how far he is willing to go (230).

After Ts'eh leaves him, Tayo braces for confrontation. Initially, only Harley and Leroy come out to find him. The three of them proceed to drink together, even though Tayo knows he should not resort to such behavior. He rationalizes the behavior by thinking that Leroy and Harley will go back and report that he is fine, that he is just another drunk Indian (and at least authorities will be satisfied with that answer). Some time in the course of the night, Tayo loses his friends. When he awakes to find them gone, he is faced with the sudden realization that they are not really his friends and that they had probably come to do him harm. His suspicion is made real when a couple of days later Leroy, Pinkie, and Emo return to the ranch site in search of

Tayo. With them is an "imprisoned" Harley, whom they have locked in the trunk of the car as punishment for "losing" Tayo. Witnessing the spectacle of the four from a safe distance, Tayo watches the three men demean and torture a powerless Harley. Finally, they all leave, with Tayo now realizing that he will never interact with them again.

Tayo does not return to Auntie's right away. He spends more time alone until he is sure he is ready to face the family. Soon after he does return, he learns that Harley and Leroy suffered a fatal car crash. Some time after that incident, Emo kills Pinkie. Exiled to California, Emo will no longer be a threat to Tayo's sanity. Now the only Laguna veteran left in this particular community, Tayo can be himself, whoever that self is. His story is no longer that of Harley or Leroy or Emo. Though he will always be linked to them in the past, how he proceeds with his future is completely left up to him.

HISTORICAL BACKGROUND

Ceremony, published in 1977, is set primarily in the latter 1940s following Tayo's return from World War II. As indicated previously, the main plotline charts Tayo in his yearlong battle with post-traumatic stress syndrome. The time setting is punctuated with flashbacks from earlier periods in Tayo's life so that the overall structure of the novel is circular rather than chronological. These earlier moments include not only the six years during which Tayo has been absent, but also prewar snippets from his childhood and adolescence.

This broad-based perspective invites a comprehensive analysis of the plight of Native Americans, particularly those who inhabit the Pueblo of Laguna Indian Reservation. Located approximately 50 miles west of Albuquerque, New Mexico, this reservation is home to one of the largest and oldest tribes in the country. It is also the site of longtime uranium mining, from roughly the early 1950s to the early 1980s. During the 30 years when the Anaconda Corporation leased 7,000 acres of the 418,000 acres of Laguna Pueblo, the lifestyle and economic circumstances of scores of Laguna people improved. During the operating years the Laguna tribal council stipulated that it would have priority over who would be employed in the mines. As a result, over 90 percent of the labor was supplied by the people of Laguna. However, when Anaconda ceased operations, it left behind an economically broken people who could not easily transfer their mining skills into other forms of gainful employment. In addition, the area suffered environmental hazards from the years of poorly monitored mining. In the mid- to late-1970s, the Laguna discovered exposure to contaminated water as a result of uranium leakage into the water supply system. The Laguna people found themselves victims of what would later be termed environmental racism, the practice whereby a racial group is exposed to hazards without any move toward accountability or compensation by the offending corporate entity.

What Leslie Marmon Silko has done in *Ceremony* is to appropriate this contemporary racialized moment (the environmental and political revelations of the 1970s) and apply it to the United States' historical treatment of Native American people. On July 16, 1945, the first atomic bomb was tested at the Trinity Site (New Mexico) after it had been created in Los Alamos, New Mexico. As with subsequent uranium drilling, the potential toxic effect on surrounding areas, particularly those inhabited by Native American peoples, would not be known for a long time. That such tests were conducted in the proximity of Native American land speaks to the low regard (racially motivated low regard) with which such people were held. *Ceremony* personalizes this fact when Tayo, after gaining some perspective on the recent past (following the healing powers of his ceremony), realizes that nuclear testing had occurred close enough to his Laguna home to cause a disturbance. Though he was away at war on that July night, Grandma tells him of her vivid memory about having to get up in the middle of the night and then witnessing a strange flash of light: "Strongest thing on this earth. Biggest explosion that ever happened—that's what the newspaper said" (245). Tayo then realizes that the site of explosion is only 300 miles to the southeast and that the site of creation is a mere 100 miles to the northeast—on land that the federal government "took from Cochiti Pueblo" (246).

Ceremony confirms allegations highlighting the atrocities visited upon Native Americans. The periodic allusion to the Bureau of Indian Affairs (BIA) reminds the reader of the United States' complicated past with Native Americans. Created in 1824 as an agency in the War Department, the BIA was charged with jurisdiction over Native American trade and settlement. In short, it was established to control all matters related to Native Americans. In the 1970s, with the emergence of the American Indian Movement, the BIA came under attack when various Native American groups expressed dissatisfaction with the organization. Since that time Native Americans have wielded more influence with the BIA, even occupying positions of leadership. The history of the BIA is also the history of the Native Americans' political journey from objectification toward agency and authority. Tayo's journey, in particular, captures this development in its linkage of past, present, and future.

LITERARY ANALYSIS

In *Ceremony,* race functions as a metaphor for exploring the conflict between confinement and liberation. Confinement is highlighted in the novel not only by Tayo's actual imprisonment during World War II, but also by the psychological trauma he has suffered as a result of that imprisonment. In many ways, Tayo is confinement personified. As a Native American who inhabits a land that has relegated Native Americans to second-class citizenship, Tayo is subjected to further oppression. As a mixed-blood Native American whose bitter and biased aunt despises his white blood, Tayo finds no real sanctuary in his home. He suffers all of society's arbitrary and offensive attempts at oppression.

Liberation is codified in the novel by the defiant natural world that resists the restrictions imposed by the so-called civilized world. In this natural world, all boundaries become blurred, absolutes are negated, and definitions of normal or abnormal are made ineffective. The very structure of the novel underscores this fact. The past penetrates the present which penetrates the future, so that time moves not along an ordered, chronological path but along a cyclical journey that has no beginning or no end (and not even any special moments of demarcation). Time moves along a fluid continuum that ultimately shatters hierarchical paradigms that would exist in precise moments (moments that would give credence and space to power/oppressed relationships). *Ceremony* is all about ritual and journeys and movement, and as long as one is engaged in the ceremony (in the journey), he is less likely to be consumed (or confined) by what would be a position of oppression. The novel is about the path to liberation.

American (i.e., white) society has physically restricted those like Tayo (the reservation while purporting to "reserve" space for the Native Americans in reality corrals them and denies their access and "possession" of other lands). This society has also sought to restrict them emotionally in order to define and objectify them. Having gone off to war and fought in defense of the United States, a traumatized Tayo and his cohorts (Harley, Leroy, Pinkie, and even Emo) have returned to a life of drunkenness, debauchery, and violence. Their emotional destruction gives rise to easy stereotypes held by whites about Native American people. Ironically, as long as the men sustain their drunken stupor and engage in useless violence against each other, the authorities have no problem with them. With this behavior, the men "justify" the negative beliefs that others harbor against them. While Tayo struggles against becoming a full emotional casualty of war, the others, especially Emo, seem to luxuriate in exhibiting the worst form of the Native American stereotype. Emo has brought his embrace of wartime violence back to peacetime. Emo carries around with him the teeth from the corpse of a Japanese soldier. They become an emblem of his warped sense of manhood. Though it pains Tayo to discover the truth about Emo's motivation and sense of self, "Tayo could hear it in his voice when he talked about the killing—how Emo grew from each killing. Emo fed off each man he killed, and the higher the rank of the dead man, the higher it made Emo" (61). Now with these teeth still in his possession, Emo defines his present identity on the destruction of another human being. Emo, of course, does not see himself as confined or brainwashed. Though he thinks he defines himself (his physical power makes him feel otherwise powerful), in reality Emo has been objectified by the white establishment and then summarily discarded. As long as Tayo interacts with those like Emo, he, too, is forever trapped in a role someone else has defined for him. In this way, the arbitrary nature of race has trapped him and left him with no other way of seeing himself or his humanity. He is violent and lost because he is Native American (by society's standards). It is his duty to self, however, to fight against that concept.

Ironically, Tayo's mixed-breed status compels him to militate against objectification. As a man positioned on the racial margin, Tayo is not clearly defined by either racial dictate (white or Native American). In this capacity, Tayo is better equipped to reject all external (societal) forms of definition. When one does not occupy one of the official racial spaces determined by society, one is denied, in essence, the comfort zone that allows him to blindly accept the racial space as the normative. Functioning on the margins, one more easily assesses the arbitrary and baseless nature of such labels, racial or otherwise. In fact, Tayo is put in the strange position of challenging the very labels that have been foisted upon him. Because Tayo has not been "protected" by any racial space, he is left to his own devices about how to cope in the world. His Native American status is worthless in the world outside the reservation; his white blood renders him worthless (to some) on the reservation. Therefore, he must carefully consider what society is trying to do to him when it ostracizes him at every turn. When he is not fully welcomed in any racial space, Tayo is, in fact, freed to create his own functional (emotional, intellectual, and psychological) space. Tayo comes to realize that defined and sanctioned racial spaces really confine and disempower those who occupy them. Without the impositions inherent in racial "occupation," Tayo is left to re-create himself more wholly.

A more complete Tayo learns to question how labels are used to entrap and brainwash (mental confinement). During his healing ceremony with Betonie, the medicine man admonishes him to interrogate all knowledge, especially such knowledge that would negatively appraise a group of people. According to Betonie, "Nothing is that simple, you don't write off all the white people, just like you don't trust all the Indians" (128). Here, Betonie insists that Tayo look beyond the labels of white and Indian. Instead, he should consider the individuals who occupy these previously determined (and imposed) racial spaces. Just because someone is labeled (restricted) as an Indian, he or she is not necessarily good, and just because someone is labeled as white, he or she is not necessarily evil. Tayo must liberate his thinking so that he can more fully assess each person and each situation. Insisting again that there are no absolutes in the world order, Betonie continues: "But don't be so quick to call something good or bad. There are balances and harmonies always shifting, always necessary to maintain.... It is a matter of transitions, you see; the changing, the becoming must be cared for closely" (130). Acknowledging such change is an act of freedom because if one expects and anticipates change, then he or she is not shocked or paralyzed (emotionally or intellectually) when said change occurs. To defy change is a foolish act which only confines one to a position of permanent irrelevance.

Still another way in which *Ceremony* addresses the conflict between freedom and confinement is in the major thematic impulse of the real versus the surreal. In the novel, the real world is represented by the rigid, oppressive social order the Auntie favors. Priding herself on her strong Christian values, Auntie defines herself by the cross she believes she must bear in trying to preserve the reputation of her family. She needs her family to serve as the model Laguna family, outpacing all others in the local vicinity of the expansive reservation. For her, Tayo's very existence is an affront to the rectitude she so sedulously strives to maintain. Though she pretends to want the perfect, morally upstanding family, Auntie really relishes the bit of shame she believes has been brought on the family by the immoral behavior of her younger sister, by the illegitimate and "mixed" birth of Tayo, and by Josiah's affair with a Mexican woman. While Tayo's mental instability offers her a new burden, it also offers Auntie a new opportunity to exhibit fortitude and resilience: "she needed a new struggle, another opportunity to show those who might gossip that she had still another unfortunate burden which proved that, above all else, she was a Christian woman" (30). Auntie's religion and her self-righteous attitude unfortunately subvert the humanity she thinks she displays. In reality, she is confined by her belief system. Instead of embracing the rapidly changing world, she tries to harness it and impose her truth on a world that is more powerful than she. Even though she once wanted Rocky to abandon the Native American ways and assimilate into the mainstream, white world (in a move that could be considered progress), she really wants him to reject what is, in essence, one ideology for another ideology in the sense that Rocky would be subjected to the dehumanizing rules of being that would suppress all individual thought and interrogation. Auntie's world, along with the world she wishes for Rocky to enter, harnesses rather than nurtures.

On the other hand, the world that Tayo attempts to enter, via his ceremony and in his return to the open spaces near the ranch, functions to defy boundaries. Even before Tayo returned home from the horrors of war, he had begun to experience a boundaryless existence. While he is fighting in the middle of a Philippine jungle, Tayo thinks he sees his Uncle Josiah, a vision which practically paralyzes him and leaves him ill-equipped to attack the enemy. In the real world, Uncle Josiah could not possibly be in the middle of the Pacific Ocean; however, in the surreal world of Tayo's imagination, many "truths" are possible. This surreal mental space makes Tayo more responsive to the natural world than he is to the "civilized" society that segregates and pigeonholes people. Uncle Josiah's presence in the jungle serves to dismantle the restrictive boundaries used to separate people by the arbitrary notion of race. When Tayo sees him, he must reconsider the Japanese soldiers (the so-called enemy) in light of Uncle Josiah's presence. As Betonie explains to Tayo much later, "The Japanese. It isn't surprising you saw him with them. You saw who they were. Thirty thousand years ago they were not strangers" (124). Tayo is confronted with seeing the Japanese as people just as he sees his Uncle Josiah as a person. Race or national boundaries notwithstanding, human beings have little difference when one penetrates the surface of their imposed identity.

The scene in which Tayo is compelled to reconsider the humanity of the Japanese soldiers recalls the scene in which Tayo and Rocky are recruited to join the war effort. The army recruiter proudly declares:

"Anyone can fight for America, even you boys. In a time of need, anyone can fight for her" (64). To two naive boys, the recruiter's words would seem welcoming and inclusive; however, to the more experienced listener, the words drip with racism and condescension. Rocky and Tayo's induction into the army and their subsequent participation in the war are rendered offensive in hindsight. Under the guise of patriotism, they are brought into the fold, but this same patriotism is without substance, existing only as another empty label which serves to divide human beings and compromise humanity. Patriotism is at once seductive and lethal. By the time that Tayo is poised to herd Uncle Josiah's cattle back to Laguna land, he better understands such propaganda and the hypocrisy that upholds it. For Tayo, the white perspective on life and power is comprised of well-crafted lies. Because such falsehoods "devoured white hearts,...for more than two hundred years white people had worked to fill their emptiness; they tried to glut the hollowness with patriotic wars and with great technology and the wealth it brought" (191). Given this revelation, Tayo is determined to complete his ceremony and restore the mental health stripped from him in the interest of further U.S. imperialism. He is being liberated when he pierces the propaganda formerly imposed on him. He must challenge the rhetoric presented to him about everything from racial identity to patriotic honor. The weaning process that he observes with the goats at the ranch is emblematic of his maturation beyond the political, cultural, and racial indoctrinations he has previously suffered. Tayo ultimately learns that "he had never been crazy. He had only seen and heard the world as it always was: no boundaries, only transitions through all distances and time" (246).

BIBLIOGRAPHY

American Indian Movement Official Web site, "History," www.aimovement.org (accessed March 5, 2004).

Barnett, Louise K., and James L. Thorson, eds. *Leslie Marmon Silko: A Collection of Critical Essays*. Albuquerque: University of New Mexico Press, 1999.

Brooks, Joanna. *American Lazarus: Religion and the Rise of African-American and Native American Literatures*. New York: Oxford University Press, 2003.

Hulan, Renee, ed. *Native North America: Critical and Cultural Perspectives*. Toronto, ON: ECW Press, 1999.

Jaskoski, Helen. *Leslie Marmon Silko: A Study of the Short Fiction.* New York: Twayne Publishers, 1998.

Silko, Leslie Marmon. *Ceremony.* New York: Penguin, 1977.

Swann, Brian, and Arnold Krupat, eds. *Recovering the Word: Essays on Native American Literature.* Berkeley: University of California Press, 1987.

Taylor, Theodore. *The Bureau of Indian Affairs.* Boulder, CO: Westview Press, 1984.

U.S. Department of Defense. *Project TRINITY, 1945–1946.* Washington, DC, 1982.

Walker, Cheryl. *Indian Nation: Native American Literature and Nineteenth-Century Nationalisms.* Durham, NC: Duke University Press, 1997.

8

Arlene J. Chai, *The Last Time I Saw Mother* (1995)

PLOT SYNOPSIS

In *The Last Time I Saw Mother* protagonist Caridad finds herself on a journey of self-discovery when her mother Thelma, in a two-sentence letter, suddenly summons her home. A resident of Sydney, Australia, for the past 10 years, Caridad is both apprehensive and eager to return to her native Manila; she suspects that the trip will mark a significant transition in her life. Because her last trip to Manila three years prior was to bury her father, she fears that Thelma's request concerns the older woman's health. Therefore, when Thelma offers no particular reason why she wants Caridad to come to Manila, the dutiful daughter leaves almost immediately for the Philippines.

Caridad's departure from Sydney is not without heartache. Recently separated from her husband Jaime, she wonders how she will explain her domestic troubles to her family. Moreover, Caridad does not relish leaving her 18-year-old daughter Marla who, albeit independent and mature, has been affected by her parents' separation. That her home life is unstable makes Caridad even more sensitive to familial connections. Going to Manila brings both relief and stress. Caridad's emotional vulnerabilities, however, make her receptive to the discoveries she will make while away from Sydney.

Upon arriving at her mother's home, Caridad is escorted upstairs to her old room. She spies a different group of maids from those she remembered on her last trip home. Knowing how exacting her mother is, Caridad understands that her mother probably intimidated her former employees. This possibility reminds Caridad once again of the personality she is about to encounter. After taking a few minutes to collect herself, Caridad ventures into her mother's dark quarters. Calling out to Thelma by calling her "Mama," Caridad is stunned when Thelma replies by stating, "No, Caridad, I am not your mama" (Chai, *The Last Time I Saw Mother*, 38).

Thelma begins to unravel a mystery that has plagued the family ever since Caridad's birth. Though she has kept the secret for so many years, in the past three years since her husband Raoul's death, Thelma has felt an urgent need to expose the truth. For over 40 years, only Thelma, her younger sister Emma, Emma's oldest daughter Ligaya, and Raoul have known the truth about Caridad's past. Appreciating the fact that she will die one day, Thelma thinks it best if Caridad learn the truth from the only mother she has known. In anticipating what will be a difficult discussion, Thelma recaps for herself moments from the past when she should have divulged the truth to her "daughter": Caridad at 17 when she begins to test her parents' authority; Caridad and Jaime announcing that they would migrate to Sydney; the young couple advancing through the stages of home ownership; and finally Raoul's death. Now, along with Emma and Ligaya, Thelma will reveal to Caridad details not only about her immediate past, but also about the more comprehensive ancestral past. Understanding that the story of the past is mainly Emma's story, she will allow her sister to talk to Caridad first.

But before the three women share their stories with her, Caridad recalls various moments from her childhood when she questioned her identity. Once, at age four, when she and friends were playing outside and her "Aunt" Emma came to visit, one of her playmates exclaimed, "It's your mama, Caridad" (58), after examining how much Caridad looked like Emma. Then at Caridad's fifth birthday party, someone in the crowd observed how much Caridad resembled Ligaya, much to Thelma's consternation and to Emma's embarrassment. Sometime thereafter, when Caridad was visiting Emma's house for Ligaya's engagement party, she happened upon a picture of Emma's deceased husband. When Caridad asked Ligaya if the man in the photograph was Ligaya's father, all Ligaya would say was "That is Papa" (65), refusing to say, "Yes, that is [my or our] Papa." Then after Marla was born and Emma and daughter Mia paid Caridad a visit in the hospital, Emma insisted on giving to Caridad her only cherished piece of jewelry, a heart-shaped pendant. Caridad could not believe that her "aunt" would not give that to one of her daughters—Ligaya, Mia, Celia, or Laura. Still, she accepted the kind offer and did not ask questions.

Now, years later, she braces herself to hear Emma's story. Arriving at Emma's home for Sunday dinner, Caridad will finally hear the truth about her background. Emma begins her story by telling of her husband Alfonso's premature death at age 39. Alfonso left Emma with six children—Ligaya, Celia, Laura, Mia, Paolo, and Miguel—and another on the way. This seventh child would be Caridad (or charity). Emma goes on to explain that while she and Alfonso enjoyed a married and family life full of love and support, they also reviewed much economic heartache as a result of the political and social upheaval which consumed their Filipino lives during World War II. Born without the benefit of the kind of family wealth that Raoul enjoyed, Alfonso was forced to work very hard to sustain his family. During the heat of World War II, Alfonso, Emma, and the children were forced to flee their Manila home and live like nomads while trying to eek out a living. At the end of the war, realizing that life in Manila would not be the same, they moved to Olongapo, where Alfonso and a partner work, to open up an ice plant. Before this venture came to fruition, however, Alfonso died. After Caridad was born three weeks later, Emma was faced with a painful decision. Because she could not feed the children she already had, she felt even more burdened with the prospect of trying to feed Caridad, too. A childless Thelma offered Emma an alternative. If Emma would relinquish Caridad to her sister, then Thelma would provide Emma's family with all of their necessities. Though initially reluctant, Emma ultimately relented. Caridad was given over to Thelma and Raoul; soon thereafter Emma and her family returned to Manila to be closer to Thelma. Emma handed over Caridad only after she suffered a nightmare that portended Caridad's death. Interpreting the dream to mean that if she kept Caridad then the child would die, a physically and emotionally drained Emma made the only choice she believed she could.

After hearing Emma's story, Caridad is then confronted with Ligaya's tale. Harboring a grudge against Thelma for all of these years, Ligaya, in an effort not to hurt Caridad, strives very hard to suppress her biases and recount an objective story. From Ligaya, Caridad learns that Alfonso was especially proud of his firstborn. He and Ligaya were practically inseparable during her childhood. Upon her fifth birthday, Alfonso bought her a piano and encouraged her musical interests. The piano quickly became Ligaya's pride and joy. Even after moving to Olongapo, Ligaya continued to play and take lessons. When Alfonso died, however, the then 15-year-old Ligaya had to end her lessons because the family could no longer afford such a luxury. The shock of her father's death was compounded by the fact that when Alfonso died, Ligaya was away on a trip to Manila that her father had instructed her not to take. As a consequence, she was burdened with intense guilt. Soon after his death, Emma sold the piano without alerting Ligaya, and then she gave Caridad to Thelma. Ligaya was overwhelmed by all of these abrupt changes. Everything in her life that once gave her pleasure had been taken from her. That her Aunt Thelma would make a bargain with Emma over her sister Caridad and that Emma would accept it completely unnerved Ligaya. Though she was angry at both Thelma and Emma, she also blamed herself for the chain of events that resulted in the disruption of the family unit: Ligaya shouldered much guilt about her absence at the time of her father's death. As well, she blamed herself for not being courageous enough to stand up to Thelma. Right after Thelma took Caridad away, Ligaya made the journey to Manila to bring Caridad back to Olongapo. Confronting her aunt fearlessly, Ligaya almost succeeded in leaving with Caridad until Thelma reminded Ligaya that the family would starve without Thelma's help, assistance she would immediately curtail if Caridad was removed. Succumbing in that moment, Ligaya left Caridad with Thelma, and soon Emma, Ligaya, and the others moved back to Manila. For years, seething with anger and resentment, Ligaya had been transformed into the kind of hardened woman she accused Thelma of being. During the seven years following Alfonso's death, Ligaya considered her life torturous and ascetic. At 22, she was pursued by the wealthy and U.S.-educated Enrique, who quickly won over Emma and the others. While Enrique had much to offer Ligaya, including his unequivocal love, Ligaya did not love him (a fact she made clear to him). Still, out of obligation to her family's well-being, she agreed to marry him. Living in the lap of luxury with four cars, a minimansion, jewelry, and servants, Ligaya had improved her station in life considerably. Still, she did not feel quite whole until she shared with Caridad the snippets from her own life that would help to make Caridad whole as well.

Finally, Caridad hears Thelma's full story. Never before had Thelma ever discussed her life prior to Caridad's birth. Anytime Caridad tried to ask her about the past, Thelma always skirted the issue. Now, however, Thelma understands that Caridad must know everything about Thelma and Raoul's life. Thelma was older than most when she and Raoul married. Already 22 when she met him, she was 23 by the time they wed. Fearing that she might not marry and feeling a sense of urgency, Thelma's parents solicited the help of her godmother Lorena to find a suitable mate. Lorena soon found the handsome and successful Raoul, a wealthy heir to the largest construction business in Manila. Though leery of her future mother-in-law, Thelma found Raoul most appealing, and he was quite taken with her. After the marriage, he initially treated her with great respect while also spending all of his free time with her dancing and dining in some of Manila's most exclusive venues. Months and then years passed without Thelma's conceiving a child, much to the in-laws' (especially the mother-in-law's) disappointment. In these ensuing years, Raoul spent more time away drinking and carousing with friends. More time elapsed without Thelma and Raoul's producing a child, when suddenly one day, Raoul came home with a baby boy, whom he convinced Thelma they should adopt. Thelma accepted the boy and worked hard to become a devoted mother. Within the year, she discovered that Angelo was actually the child Raoul fathered with a paramour. Angry and hurt, Thelma returned to her parents' house, whereupon her mother insisted that she return home to husband and child. Thelma's mother assured her that if she returned, forgave Raoul (while saying nothing accusatory to him), and embraced her role as mother, all would be well. Thelma proceeded in this vein until Angelo's first birthday when the baby's natural mother suddenly appeared to reclaim her son. In an emotionally charged scene over which she assumed control (even wresting it from the mother-in-law and Raoul), Thelma, knowing that the mother wanted only money, handed over Angelo, whereupon the exploitative woman returned the baby and stormed out. From that moment on, Raoul gained a new respect for (and increasingly suffered a slight fear of) Thelma. A few weeks later, unfortunately, Angelo became ill and died of meningitis. Yet again, Thelma and Raoul were left childless. Deciding that they needed a new start, Raoul and Thelma moved out of his parents' house. Thinking that they would live out the remainder of their lives in peace, the couple resign themselves to a permanent empty nest. However, when Thelma visited Emma after Alfonso's death and found her in such dire straits, she could not help but to prod Emma and even browbeat her to relinquish Caridad to her. Though she admits in the present that she probably acted insensitively, she hopes that in the end, all lives have been affected positively. As she explains to Caridad, "I did buy you but, although it was not the right thing to have done, I like to think of it now as a wrong act that has led to many right things in the end" (310).

Having relieved herself of all the secrets without losing Caridad, Thelma, now livelier than she has been in years, decides to throw her daughter a farewell party. All of Caridad's cousins (siblings) are invited to Thelma's house. When Ligaya comes, she and Thelma achieve a new peace between them. In these moments of family harmony, Caridad realizes that she and Jaime have much to discuss upon her return. She is determined to salvage her marriage and her nuclear family. A few months after her return, Caridad receives the call that every adult child knows he or she will get one day. Thelma has passed away peacefully in bed while perusing old and new photographs. Given the recent chain of events which have made Caridad whole again, Thelma's passing is not a sad affair. It is simply another chapter in the longer story that Caridad will share with her daughter one day soon. The story will shape the identities of generations to come.

HISTORICAL BACKGROUND

The novel is set around two significant events in Philippine history: the Japanese Occupation of the Philippines during World War II and the overthrow of the Ferdinand Marcos regime in 1986. Caridad, who was born in 1946 and is now age 40, serves as the main link between these two moments in history. As both Emma and Thelma share with Caridad, when the Japanese attacked the Philippines at the end of 1941, life for Filipino citizens changed forever. The course that Caridad's life takes is affected directly by the ensuing social, political, and economic upheaval. Even before her birth, racial and international strife define what will be her Filipino homeland.

During World War II, the Japanese enforced an oppressive propaganda program. Displeased with the influence that the United States had on Filipino life and culture, the Japanese insisted that all parts of Asia should be ruled only by Asians and that anyone of Asian descent must prove himself or herself to be a proud Asian. During this time, Filipino writers who once wrote in English began writing in Tagalog because the new rulers recognized only two official languages, Japanese and Tagalog. The Japanese were determined to wipe out any trace of European or U.S. influence. For three years, the Filipino people suffered under Japanese rule. No doubt the most infamous of Japanese misdeeds was the Bataan Death March. In April 1942, over 70,000 U.S. and Filipino prisoners of war were forced to march from the southern end of the Bataan Peninsula for over 60 miles to Camp O'Donnell. Many prisoners were beaten, starved, and executed. Approximately 55,000 completed the trek; the others died or escaped into the jungle. While the Japanese ostensibly tried to take back the Philippines for Asian interests, they inflicted cruel acts on the very people they purported "to save." Supposedly, they were race loyal (to the general Asian community); in reality their race consciousness was highly flawed.

Ironically, the Japanese treatment of the local Filipinos was more consistent with the behavior of a colonial power than it was with the actions of a "savior." During the heat of the Japanese Occupation, Alfonso comments to Emma about the similarities between the Japanese behavior and earlier colonial interferences: "The Japanese rule now so it is their actions we remember. But the Spaniards were just as bad. And the Americans, too.... Why should one country rule over another? The Spaniards, the Americans and the Japanese have no business here. This is not a Filipino war" (124). This war not only caused intensified racial stratifications but also intensified racial strife. The Filipinos, according to Emma, increased their envy of both Spaniards and Chinese. The Filipinos "feared and envied" the Spaniards because of their economic might and their political clout; they "hated and envied" (109) the Chinese because of their rapid economic success and adaptation in the Philippines. Emma and Alfonso, though ancestrally considered Chinese, have more in common with native Filipinos because of their economic confinement. This oppressed status makes them more Filipino than Chinese; this cross-racial identity makes them more aware of racial conflict and more sensitive to the importance of cross-racial collaboration and support. The ancestral identity is one issue, while their economic identity is a practical concern that registers more deeply with them.

It is this economic concern, after Alfonso's untimely death, that changes Caridad's life forever. When Emma finds she cannot care for her family, she feels as though she has no choice but to relinquish Caridad to the manipulative and wealthy Thelma who, now in the World War II aftermath, assumes the attitude of a haughty Spaniard. Rather than acting like a sister to Emma and offering her help without condition, Thelma acts as an oppressive force (one tinged with racism) who induces guilt and shame in order convince Emma to give up Caridad.

Now 40 years later, Caridad returns to Manila in 1986 in the aftermath of yet another period of political unrest. This time, unlike her birth on the heels of World War II and the Japanese insurgence, Caridad's arrival comes just as the Filipino people strive to reinstate legitimate Filipino authority on the national front and restore integrity to government. Two months prior, the People's Power Movement overthrew the Marcos regime and swore in Corazon Aquino as the new president of the Philippines. While this revolution was undertaken with great promise for a better domestic circumstance for the Filipino people, change will come very slowly. As Caridad observes her homeland for the first time since she came to bury Raoul three years earlier, she realizes that Jaime was right in his assessment about the situation there. She notices that all of "the vendors and beggars roaming the streets" are "without exception" Filipino (32). In the 40 years since her birth, Filipinos have not fared well, in part because, according to Jaime, "We have been owned so long we don't remember who we are. We think this is the way to be. We have become so accepting and indifferent to oppression" (33). Jaime also concludes that the Filipino people's nonchalance about their condition is their acceptance of oppression from external forces. Somehow, when they are oppressed by people who are different from them, they simply capitulate: "We bow to four hundred years and more of colonial rule, suffering a thousand indignities, whereas all we needed to shake free of this state of servitude was a taste of homemade dictatorship" (33), and still that rebellion erupted only after 21 years of Marcos dictatorship. Race is an interesting phenomenon: people are more likely to accept abuse interracially than they are intraracially.

From 1986 to the novel's publication in 1995, life for native Filipinos had not radically improved. The Aquino presidency was marred by administrative infighting, coup attempts, and continued political and economic disillusionment. Even beyond the term of Aquino's presidency, which ended in 1992, thousands of human rights violations were reported. The hope that came with the Aquino rise to power was soon deflated. Mia's words to Caridad, upon retrieving her from the airport, ring true: "Too soon to tell, Caridad; you can't dismantle years of corrupt bureaucracy overnight. Even now there's already so much in-fighting and confusion.... I'd hate to be Cory [Corazon Aquino].... The people have such high hopes, such unrealistic expectations, that I'm afraid they'll be disappointed" (28–29). With a post-1992 hindsight, *The Last Time I Saw Mother* understands that domestic stability—political, economic, and racial—will remain forever elusive.

LITERARY ANALYSIS

In *The Last Time I Saw Mother* the search for Caridad's familial identity also encompasses for Caridad an understanding of her place in the highly racialized society of her Philippine homeland. Race and racism are subsumed in the protagonist's search for emotional whole-ness. As the familial oppression that Caridad feels is tantamount to the more generalized racial oppression that impacts Manila and its envi-rons, her attempt to know and to defeat past family demons is also an attempt to battle the racism that lurks underneath Philippine life. The dominant theme in this novel concerns exposing the false or arbitrary boundaries erected to oppress, corral, and confine, while shedding light on human truth and its liberating forces.

Long before Thelma, Emma, and Ligaya tell Caridad the truth about her past, Caridad had often wondered about her identity. Be-cause there had been clues all along that something was amiss in her life, Caridad always felt incomplete: "By never knowing my past, I was never sure of who I was. Because mine was missing, I never felt whole" (56). She was consumed with the paradoxical feeling of both belonging to Raoul and Thelma and feeling somewhat estranged from them. Her questions about her identity, interestingly enough, assume a kind of racial interrogation as well: "Often I would look in the mir-ror and try to make out my features. Whose eyes were these, whose nose, whose lips, whose face. I had Mama's hair. The rest I thought was part Mama, part Papa so that I resembled neither one of them in a definite way. A mix" (62). On the one hand, these are the natural musings of a child, any child, who detects no discernible similarities between herself and her parents. On the other hand, the questions be-come more racially charged when one assesses the subtle yet poignant details concerning both Thelma and Raoul's complexions. Caridad describes Thelma as being "golden brown" (58), while Thelma re-ports (from her godmother) that Raoul is "quite dark for a Chinese" (245). Caridad is different from her parents not only in terms of facial composition, but also in terms of color. Even her childhood friends once noted, when her "aunt" paid the family a visit, that Emma looked like Caridad's mother. Caridad is grappling not only with the difference between her and her parents, but also with the notion of racial mixture. While she uses the term "mix" to suggest that she's a mixture of both Thelma and Raoul that blurs any distinct traits from either, she is also (perhaps subconsciously) suggesting that she is a mix of different family lines (Emma's and Thelma's) or that she is of racially mixed blood. The ways in which these different threads of dis-cussion are woven throughout the novel are many and varied.

That Caridad is consumed with race on some level and that this at-tention is directly related to her concern for familial identity is evident when she recalls the birth of her daughter Marla (her link to the future, just as Thelma and Emma are her links to the past). In describing the newborn Marla, Caridad notes, "She was a beautiful baby. She was not fair-skinned but she had a beautiful face" (70). Here Caridad implies that despite the baby's dark features, she is a still an appealing child, though she hints that she would have preferred a child who possessed Caridad's lighter features. It seems as though Caridad is tacitly echoing the words of Thelma's godmother years earlier who, after divulging the information about Raoul's dark complexion, declares that such a feature "is not bad in a man" (245). The comment suggests that darkness is unacceptable in a woman, though it might be tolerated in a man. The point here is that as Caridad systematically reconciles with her past, she must also face the demons of race and color prejudice. Even though she thinks she does not harbor any racial bias (because she has married the racially mixed Jaime and produced a daughter even more racially mixed), she must confront the fact that she has assumed some of the notions of Chinese purity expressed in previous generations of her family.

Marla's very presence in the novel subverts the notion of racial absolutes and, in so doing, thwarts historical oppressive forces. The Philippines has long been comprised of four major ethnic (or national) groups: native Filipinos, Spaniards, Chinese, and Americans (meaning European-American). The Spaniards colonized the Philippine islands for over 300 years and assumed political and economic power, while the Chinese came later and, exploiting their business acumen, carved out a respectable niche for themselves. Then the Americans arrived with new ideas on education. The Filipinos were left with the least control over their physical and cultural space. Clear lines of demarcation were in effect. While some intermarrying certainly occurred, particularly among the Chinese and Filipinos, racial lines would remain clearly defined. Marla, with her multiracial persona and independent bearing, defies any attempt at categorization. As she happily admits, in commenting on her unique identity, her Chinese-Filipino-Spanish heritage, "To confuse the issue, I'm not only Manila-born, convent-school-educated, speak English and Tagalog plus a bit of Chinese and curse fluently in Spanish, but now I reside in Australia as well" (8). Marla, who looks like a punk rock musician as she hones her skills as a classical pianist, confounds the perspective of those from earlier generations who, like Thelma, despise "things that grow wild and do not belong" (19). That Marla dominates the opening segment of the novel suggests, in part, that she represents the social and cultural perspective that Caridad must achieve. Caridad even describes Marla as being more like a mother to Caridad and Caridad as being more like the obedient daughter. Marla represents the new lessons that the family must learn about race and about survival, not just in Manila, but also in the broader global space.

Being a composite of various ethnicities, Marla personifies a new multidimensional identity forging ahead at the end of the twentieth century. Her ethnic makeup and her transnational identity afford her a more sophisticated, more progressive view of people and their cultural space. Though Caridad, early in the novel, believes that "migrants," like her nuclear family, "are people who are never whole, never completely in one place" and that theirs "is a fractured existence" (17), Marla's outlook on life and her response to being a Philippine native living in Australia belie this perspective. One is fractured only if one accepts external definitions of self and requires external validation or affirmation. Instead of being fractured, migrants (translate: multiethnic, race-conscious, and highly adaptable individuals) celebrate and embrace diversity in all of its facets. For them, the family unit, neighborhood unit, community unit, or national unit is not whole without differing parts.

Thelma relates (and further explains) this sentiment when she describes the young Raoul to Caridad. Detailing for her daughter how Raoul changed and revealed the more redemptive aspects of his personality after the arrival of Angelo, Thelma declares that "people are made of many parts. Some parts come out early in life and fade with the years, some parts last till we die, and there are those parts that come out later" (284). While Thelma is specifically discussing personality traits, her words also register more comprehensively. Caridad is made up of many parts, some of which she has only recently been made aware of. As a physical being, she is made up of Emma and Alfonso; as a psychological, emotional, and spiritual being, she has been influenced by Thelma and Raoul. Caridad's composite identity mirrors the ethnic diversity of her immediate family unit. Jaime, though at heart a Filipino, is a product of Spanish, Chinese, and Filipino blood. As aforementioned, Marla benefits from this mixed ancestry because it allows her to see the world more fully, from as many different perspectives as possible.

When Caridad faces the truth about her actual heritage (that it is with Emma and not just with Thelma), she opens the possibility for acknowledging other truths. As Emma states, when she is divulging past secrets to Caridad, "Telling the truth is like that, it is much like telling a lie—one leads to another" (85). When forced to consider her

Philippine home and her past with the detachment of time and physical space, Caridad is better equipped to acknowledge the keen racial and ethnic demarcations and delineations that Jaime has often pointed out before. Now, however, she understands how race figures in on every social, political, or even domestic concern one may confront. By bridging the topic of familial heritage with racial impulses, *The Last Time I Saw Mother* exposes very clearly the core of human interaction.

BIBLIOGRAPHY

Asia Society Official Web site, "Social Issues," www.asiasource.org (accessed March 6, 2004).

Back to Bataan, "Bataan Death March," Rick Peterson, www.bataansurvivor.com (accessed March 6, 2004).

Chai, Arlene. *The Last Time I Saw Mother.* New York: Fawcett, 1995.

Delmendo, Sharon. *The Star-Entangled Banner: One Hundred Years of America in the Philippines.* New Brunswick, NJ: Rutgers University Press, 2004.

Ephraim, Frank. *Escape to Manila: From Nazi Tyranny to Japanese Terror.* Urbana: University of Illinois Press, 2003.

Go, Julian, and Anne L. Foster, eds. *The American Colonial State in the Philippines: Global Perspectives.* Durham, NC: Duke University Press, 2003.

Rodell, Paul A. *Culture and Customs of the Philippines.* Westport, CT: Greenwood Press, 2002.

9

Nora Okja Keller, *Fox Girl* (2002)

PLOT SYNOPSIS

Nora Okja Keller's *Fox Girl* charts the development of Hyun Jin, a
Korean girl, from age six to early adulthood as she grows up in the aftermath of the Korean War. Self-conscious because of a prominent facial birthmark, Hyun Jin has compensated for this imperfection by
being the top student in her class and by lording her academic suc-
cesses over her less gifted classmates. Hyun Jin takes special pride also
in the fact that her mother and father own a business and can supply
her with necessities when most of her peers suffer from deep poverty.
She believes that the classmates who ridicule her do so not just because of her birthmark, but also because of their jealousy about her
better economic circumstances.

Hyun Jin's only close friend is Sookie, a downtrodden girl whose
mother Duk Hee earns money to raise Sookie by working as a prostitute serving U.S. GIs. Others in the community look down upon Duk
Hee and Sookie, but Hyun Jin befriends Sookie, in part because
Sookie is almost as smart as she is and also because most people consider the dark-skinned Sookie to be uglier than Hyun Jin. As Sookie is
most often the recipient of taunts and insults, Hyun Jin is shielded
from the kinds of comments that would be directed at her were Sookie
not present. Theirs is sometimes a strained alliance, yet neither has
anyone else on whom to depend. The girls spend most of their free
time together, either doing homework or wandering about the town
of Chollak, observing happenings in America Town, the area of Chol-

lak where American soldiers reside and where bars and brothels serve their needs.

While Hyun Jin's father always treats Sookie kindly, her mother despises Sookie and Hyun Jin's friendship with the girl. Believing Sookie to be "tainted" by Duk Hee's career choice, Hyun Jin's mother would rather her daughter not associate with Sookie, lest Hyun Jin suffer moral taint. Defying her mother's wishes, Hyun Jin not only maintains her relationship with Sookie, but also pays a weekly visit to Sookie's house to spend time with Duk Hee. On Thursdays, Duk Hee does not work because she must honor her contract with authorities and undergo a checkup at the clinic. After school, the girls go to Duk Hee, who instructs them on the ways of world, particularly men and the importance of sexual protection. Because she gains the kind of knowledge she would never acquire at home, Hyun Jin looks forward to these visits.

The plot is set in motion on one particular Thursday when the girls go to Sookie's house and find Duk Hee missing. Worried about her mother, Sookie convinces Hyun Jin to join her in searching for Duk Hee. Reasoning that they should first inquire at the clinic, her last known destination, the two girls venture for the first time to this facility that caters to the prostitutes of America Town. Though the doctor there does not remember Duk Hee specifically, as he attends to so many different women, he informs the girls that if Duk Hee did not pass her medical exams she was more than likely sent to a quarantined environment, known as the Monkey House, where she would be required to stay until her condition clears up. For the next several weeks, Sookie is left to fend for herself. Hyun Jin does what she can to supply Sookie with food, taking her breakfast treats every morning before school.

Sookie, however, still suffers hunger, and because of the added stress of being alone, she becomes physically ill and almost delusional one day at school. The teacher allows Hyun Jin to escort her home and to take care of her, an opportunity that Hyun Jin appreciates because she can help her friend even more without her mother's knowledge. From this point on, the relationship between the two begins to change, as Hyun Jin, who has always thought of herself as Sookie's intellectual and emotional superior, begins to see a more conniving and resourceful Sookie. While at the apartment that Sookie shares with Duk Hee, Hyun Jin discovers a healthy stash of U.S. food products. Miffed because she has been stealing food from her parents' store and the kitchen to feed Sookie on most mornings, Hyun Jin questions

Sookie about what Hyun Jin perceives as the girl's deceit. Sookie divulges that a few days back, Duk Hee's most recent GI client came in search of Duk Hee, and when he found Sookie there without any food, he bought supplies and enough food to last Sookie for a while. But Sookie, more concerned about Duk Hee than about herself, wants to save the food for Duk Hee's return. Unfazed by Sookie's story, Hyun Jin rips open the various packages of U.S. food and devours as much as she can.

When after several weeks Duk Hee does not come back, Sookie decides to go in search of her, and she convinces Hyun Jin to go with her. But because the girls do not know where the Monkey House is, they are forced to ask their nemesis/friend Lobetto (a half-Korean, half-black youth) to take them there. Knowing that when Sookie finds her mother more than likely Duk Hee will give Sookie her money for safe keeping, Lobetto agrees to take them if Sookie will share some of the proceeds with him. When they find Duk Hee, she turns over the money to Sookie, and she also asks Hyun Jin to ask her father to take Sookie in until Duk Hee can return. When Hyun Jin expresses her doubt about that possibility, Duk Hee reiterates that Hyun Jin is to ask her father. On the journey back Hyun Jin wonders why Duk Hee is so insistent about her request and why she believes that Hyun Jin's father would even consider it.

Hyun Jin never makes the request because she is sure of what the answer will be. When Duk Hee first departed, Hyun Jin asked her parents if Sookie might stay with them, a question that sent her mother into a rage and resulted in her parents engaging in a heated exchange, snippets from which Hyun Jin could barely hear. Instead of suffering through a similar spectacle, Hyun Jin simply puts Sookie off every time she asks if Hyun Jin's father will help. After so many days of this response, suddenly one day Sookie simply stops coming to school.

Several months pass, and one day Hyun Jin comes home to hear her father in deep conversation with a woman, whose voice she soon recognizes as Duk Hee. Too focused on their discussion, the adults do not notice Hyun Jin. Duk Hee pleads with Hyun Jin's father to allow Hyun Jin to go to Sookie and beg the girl to return to Duk Hee and to school. Hyun Jin's father refuses to allow his daughter to get involved, and when he realizes Hyun Jin is there listening, he insists that she leave the adults to finish their conversation. Not until Hyun Jin finds Lobetto later does she learn that Sookie has taken up prostitution, too, and that she is living in another apartment with Hyun Jin's former boyfriend, a black American named Chazu (Charles).

Upon visiting Sookie, Hyun Jin finds that Chazu has stocked the apartment with every luxury that Sookie could want. However, Sookie is very lonely because Chazu has ordered her not to sell her body anymore. Though he continues to come and go as he pleases, Sookie cannot move about freely. Happy to have her friend back, Sookie hosts miniparties for Hyun Jin and Lobetto during the next few weeks. Soon after the two (now teenage) girls reunite, Sookie informs Hyun Jin that they are not just friends, but that they are, in fact, half-sisters. Shocked and a bit confused, Hyun Jin goes in search of Duk Hee, who now lives on prostitute's row in America Town. Duk Hee explains to Hyun Jin that Duk Hee is her mother but that the man whom she has always known as her father is her biological father. When her parents married, they discovered that the "mother" could not have children, so they, much to the mother's dismay, called upon Duk Hee (whom the father had known since childhood) to conceive and then carry his child. Now Hyun Jin understands why the woman she has always thought to be her mother has treated her so poorly for all these years. Hyun Jin cannot understand how Duk Hee could so easily relinquish her own biological child. Still, she is happy to know the truth about her past.

When Hyun Jin's parents discover that she has been in contact again with Sookie and Duk Hee, they, at the "mother's" insistence, banish her from the house. Hyun Jin is forced to move in with Lobetto and his mean-spirited mother. Lobetto has fashioned himself to be a "broker" of prostitutes, and soon he will expect Hyun Jin to earn her keep. Still a virgin, Hyun Jin relents to Lobetto's demand and finds herself made the sexual toy of three GIs, who use her body in unimaginable ways. Over one month later, Hyun Jin discovers she is pregnant. Still suffering from the harsh treatment of Lobetto's mother, Hyun Jin, though feeling like she is a burden, is happy to know that the child she is carrying is at least someone whom she can truly love and who will love her in return. She becomes attached to the emergent being almost immediately. Several days after she discovers she is pregnant, however, Hyun Jin suffers a painful miscarriage. She firmly believes that the miscarriage is the result of ingesting the herbal tea that Lobetto's mother insisted she drink. Hyun Jin is devastated by the loss of her child.

In the meantime, Sookie tires of being left alone, and when she discovers that Chazu has been "dating" other women, she confronts him, and soon thereafter, they part ways. Ultimately, the now pregnant Sookie must also move in with Lobetto. Hyun Jin is happy that a child will soon join the "family," even though there is barely enough now to feed the four adults. Throughout the early stages of her pregnancy, Sookie threatens to abort the fetus. Hyun Jin pleads with her to keep the baby, even promising Sookie payment if she will carry it to term.

Still reeling from her first sexual encounter, Hyun Jin decides she must overcome her disgust and start earning money the only way she knows how. She starts performing at Club Foxa, where she engages in exotic dance, lewd sex acts, and continued prostitution. After Sookie gives birth to Myu Myu, Hyun Jin also assumes responsibility for the care of the infant, Sookie refusing to exhibit any maternal concern. Hyun Jin is forced to take the baby to the club and to pay the cook to watch over her.

Quite successful as a performer, Hyun Jin's trademark is her willingness to do anything on stage that other girls will not do. After several weeks on the job, she is offered a chance to go to Hawaii to work in a similar club there. Mrs. Yoon, a no-nonsense businesswoman, offers what amounts to indentured servitude. The cunning club owner will finance Hyun Jin's transportation to and housing in Hawaii, and the girl will work for Mrs. Yoon for a specified number of years. Believing she must do whatever she can to "escape" Korea and enter the paradise she thinks the United States to be, Hyun Jin is determined to make this trip happen.

Hyun Jin's initial plan is to relocate to Hawaii, work hard, and then earn enough money to send for Myu Myu. In order to solidify this plan, Hyun Jin, without revealing her intentions, tries to urge Sookie to take more of an interest in the child so that Myu Myu will be left in good care until Hyun Jin can send for her. Hyun Jin soon discovers that Sookie has made her own plans to go to Hawaii and work for Mrs. Yoon.

With her plan somewhat thwarted, Hyun Jin decides that if she and Sookie are going, they must also take Myu Myu with them, even though Mrs. Yoon will be furious. Sookie does not support this latest plan, firmly believing that the baby will prevent them from working like they must in order to end their indebtedness to Mrs. Yoon in a timely fashion. So determined not to take the baby, Sookie even tries to drown her.

Hyun Jin prevents the murder, and soon the three fly to Hawaii. As to be expected, Mrs. Yoon is incensed at what she considers the girls' impertinence at bringing a baby. Hyun Jin promises that Myu Myu will not prevent them from working. However, after a few weeks of leaving Myu Myu alone at night and running herself ragged trying to walk back and forth from the club to the apartment to check on the baby, Mrs. Yoon fires her and Hyun Jin is forced to leave.

With nowhere to go and with Sookie refusing to accompany them, Hyun Jin and Myu Myu go in search of an estranged uncle (her "mother's" brother) who lives in a nearby town. Upon arriving there, they find that he is long gone. Geraldine, a kindly neighbor who oversees a plant nursery, takes the two of them in. The novel ends, when five years later, Hyun Jin is still there making a life for herself by helping Gerry and educating Myu Myu (now called Maya) on the geographic and cultural wonders of the United States. All of Hyun Jin's hopes rest with the innocent and loving child.

HISTORICAL BACKGROUND

Fox Girl presents in vivid detail one aspect of U.S. occupation in South Korea following the Korean War (1950–1953). This war ensued on the heels of World War II, when in 1945 the Korean peninsula was divided into two regions, North Korea and South Korea, with the Soviet Union supporting factions in the north and the United Nations-backed United States supporting (and protecting) interests in the south. Fighting erupted on the border between the two regions in 1949, and in 1950 when North Korea invaded South Korea, the United States, along with other allies, entered the fray that would end three years later with millions of soldiers and civilians perishing. Though a cease-fire was declared on July 27, 1953, tensions in the region have never subsided. To the present day, war could erupt there at any time. After the Korean War, the United States established more military bases around the world, increasing the number created following World War II.

With the Korean War officially over, some soldiers (like Lobetto's father) returned home, leaving behind the children born out of their liaisons with Korean women. *Fox Girl* strives to examine the aftermath of these acts of irresponsibility not only by the men themselves, but also by a military that all but endorsed such behavior. Still, after the war, a widespread U.S. presence in South Korea was retained in order to maintain the peace, and enlistees found themselves with ample leisure time. By the 1960s setting of the novel, many soldiers pass their time by frequenting (Korean) government-sponsored prostitution houses, where Korean women are exploited when they engage in the only gainful employment available to them. Some of these same women have endured a lifetime of exploitation, from as early as World War II, when the Japanese invaded Korea, kidnapped Korean boys to serve in their military, and abused Korean girls for whatever pleasure they wanted. Duk Hee tells of the torture her family suffered when she was a young girl in the north. Her personal history is also the recent history of Korea. After World War II, she and Hyun Jin's father make their way south (where the "good" Americans are in control) in search of a better life. Still, several years later, she finds herself suffering economic and sexual exploitation at the hands of the Korean government and the U.S. military. Moreover, she is blamed for her activities in general and for her "friendliness" with the black GIs in particular. Hers is a story completely enmeshed in the political, racial, and militaristic complexities of this global history.

Fox Girl exposes various racial tensions that plagued Korea during this period. In the many camp towns (U.S. military areas established to maintain peace) that punctuated the Korean landscape, racial divisions were commonplace. These so-called America Towns were hotbeds of segregation, with racial strife between white GIs and black GIs intensifying. Because white soldiers outnumbered black enlistees, more bars and prostitutes catered to them. Yet when black soldiers and the women who "entertained" them ventured into white areas or establishments, they risked physical abuse.

Koreans reenacted the racism that plagued the United States, adopting narrow-minded white views about race and racial interaction. As a result, the women (like Duk Hee) who befriended black GIs were ostracized, while the children who often resulted from these sexual entanglements were cast aside as neither American nor Korean. *Fox Girl* sheds light on this signal moment in both United States and Korean history.

The novel covers a six-year period, from roughly 1963 to 1969, when the United States is witnessing rapid change with regard to race. The historical backdrop is established in *Fox Girl* when Hyun Jin recalls an important incident from five years earlier: Lobetto's receiving a letter from his black American father. In the letter, James Robert Williams tells his son about the recent March on Washington and the crowd which he describes as a "river of humanity." The event has given Lobetto's father hope that one day the United States will allow him to advance so that he can bring Lobetto (age 12 in 1963) to his paternal homeland. That the United States is being forced to reckon with her racial hypocrisy (concerning civil rights) at the same time that she is foisting upon Korean people her fully entrenched racist attitudes provides the most compelling example of narrative tension in the novel. While the United States ostensibly entered warfare with Korea to bring to that foreign land the spirit of freedom and liberty for the Korean people, it has also deposited there the diseases of segregation and prejudice.

As would be expected, the half-black, half-Korean Lobetto suffers in the crossfire. That he is forced to resort to pimping his mother and friends is offensive in and of itself. Even more disturbing is the fact that he must risk his life when he decides to advance his economic standing by "marketing" to white GIs and breaking the tacit rule that a "black" person not cross over into the white section of America Town. Racism not only oppresses people socially and economically, but also punishes them for trying to eek out a living beyond such arbitrarily imposed limitations.

LITERARY ANALYSIS

Fox Girl addresses how race impacts both economic and emotional survival. The novel exposes the extreme measures many are forced to adopt in order to cope in a society that would rather ignore or dispose of them. While the connection between race (racism) and survival is not a unique concept, *Fox Girl* examines the insidious ways in which U.S. notions of race (and the attendant racism) can invade another culture, in this case, the Korean culture.

U.S. culture (along with its various racial ills) has encroached upon Korean space in two very specific ways: (1) With the invasion of U.S. products and media images, Koreans have been made to feel inferior and even ugly, and (2) Koreans have embraced the notion of racial hatred in their castigation of anything black and in their mistreatment of the mixed-race offspring of black and Korean relationships. The second behavior is pursued in response to the first issue. As is true so often in oppressed-oppressor relationships, in order for the oppressed to feel better about themselves, they, ironically, adopt the same behaviors of their oppressors and set out to oppress someone else. In this case, since white America has bombarded the Korean space with various notions of white American superiority, making Koreans feel insecure, the Koreans then join white America in belittling anyone or anything even remotely black.

Commenting on that first transformation experienced by Koreans, with the arrival of U.S. influences, Hyun Jin records how Koreans began to view themselves differently once they were indoctrinated by

U.S. values: "When the Americans first ventured off base and into our neighborhoods, we thought they...were ugly.... Slowly, though, we began to view their features as desirable, developing a taste for large noses, double lids, and cow eyes just as we had learned to crave the chocolate candy and cakes we had once thought sweet as dirt" (Keller, *Fox Girl*, 14). Even though Hyun Jin's (legal) mother considers everything from the United States to be "whore's rubbish" (11), many in Hyun Jin's generation are transformed by the U.S. presence. Hyun Jin offers a keen analysis of the process that compels her (and the others so influenced) to shift from seeing the Korean culture as the center (as occupying the subject position) to viewing it as something alien or other, with the superior U.S. culture rightfully becoming the "centered" benchmark by which Korean culture must be judged and evaluated. That she links the seduction of U.S. products with the emotional transformation whereby she, Sookie, and others begin to define the European body as beautiful substantiates the fact that such cultural intrusions are often so intoxicating that the native residents quickly lose sight of what they once held dear. That a group of people could define a body type as ugly during one moment of observation and then define it as "desirable" in the next is a testament to the persuasive powers of racialized propaganda.

Such propaganda projects onto an unknowing (Korean) culture not only a warped sense of U.S. superiority, but also a distorted portrait of the true United States. The result is, of course, a false sense of reality that, once born, perpetuates the dissemination of inaccurate and fallacious information that unwitting recipients accept as truth. On another occasion, Hyun Jin recalls once when Lobetto is sharing some of his insights about the United States (as relayed to him via a letter from his father). He indicates to Hyun Jin that in the United States, many people (i.e., people of color) look like him. His comment, however, leaves Hyun Jin perplexed and a bit confused, given her (albeit limited) understanding of the United States' racial makeup: "I kept my mouth shut even though I wondered if that was the case, then why did all the American magazines feature light-skinned girls? I supposed it was possible that in America the men were colored differently than the women" (97). In her innocent and naive response, Hyun Jin reveals the fact that U.S. (popular culture) propaganda would feature only white women (especially in this 1960s time period). Because of such limitations, persons abroad, like Hyun Jin, are led to believe that only whites make up the United States' population or that blacks comprise a negligible percentage. The resultant belief is that if whites completely and totally dominate U.S. culture, then it is these same whites whom the Koreans should strive to emulate. The Korean psyche is further shaped by the white American perspective.

As noted earlier, the result of such influence is that the Korean mindset is positioned in opposition to black humanity. In short, Koreans are encouraged to adopt whiteness as the preferred social perspective, while objectifying blackness. When Hyun Jin and Sookie, for the first time as young girls, find a black GI sleeping in Sookie's apartment, they sidle up to him like he is the strangest phenomenon. As Hyun Jin describes, they lean over "to study" this man whose color reminds her of "the underbelly of [a] black pig," with Sookie "[poking] at him with the corner of her writing tablet," whereupon he greets them "like a trained monkey" (12). Already, Sookie and Hyun Jin have been so indoctrinated by racist notions that they consider this man, this American, no more than an object because he is black. Such racist notions pervade this small Korean community. Hyun Jin and Sookie refer to the black soldiers as darkies. Even Sookie and Lobetto are ridiculed for their darker complexions. Striving so hard to be more American, these Koreans become the best "Americans" they can be by belittling and objectifying the black men whom they encounter.

Perhaps the greatest casualties of racism are the children who are exploited and practically discarded because of their racial makeup. Those like Lobetto, whose father is a black GI, are denied entry into the schools with the other Korean children. Instead, they must attend a specially established school for "children of GI whores" (77). In this school, they are encouraged to deny their Korean heritage when they suffer further indoctrination into all things American. As a result, they are made to feel as though they occupy a kind of "no man's land." They are not fully Korean (as they are daily reminded), yet they cannot move to that great United States to which they increasingly feel a strong connection. In this way, they are made invisible and rootless.

In order to survive in this hostile environment, those like Sookie and Lobetto (and eventually Hyun Jin) must pursue the only means available to them. While Lobetto pimps his mother and sometimes Hyun Jin, both Sookie and Hyun Jin work as "entertainers" at Club Foxa. They seduce soldiers into buying more food and drinks, while also offering the men various forms of sexual gratification. Fully sanctioned by local authorities, these practices further victimize the societal throwaways by placing them in compromising circumstances, while at the same time society (represented by those like Hyun Jin's legal parents) condemns them for their behaviors.

In fact, Hyun Jin's (legal) mother argues that Dee Huk is immoral because of her "choice" of work and that Sookie and Hyun Jin are immoral because of their mixed blood (she believes/suspects that Hyun Jin is really the product of an affair that Dee Huk had with a black soldier). She refuses to consider the fact that Sookie and Hyun Jin are forced to survive in the only way they know how. Instead, the mother relies solely on her own philosophy that "Blood will tell" (125), whereby she means that the non-Korean blood that flows through Sookie and Hyun Jin will always reveal itself in their unsavory behaviors. In other words, the girls are innately evil; they cannot help but to engage in and enjoy their illicit actions.

Though her mother sees Hyun Jin as only a product of her "natural" inclinations, symbolized in the dark birthmark that scars Hyun Jin's face, Hyun Jin wishes to advance beyond the station that Korean life has determined for her. Like the fox girl from the lore of her Korean ancestors, Hyun Jin wants to transcend the present and achieve the impossible, transforming herself into a being better equipped to confront whatever racial, geographical, or gendered obstacle placed before her.

BIBLIOGRAPHY

American Battle Monuments Commission, "History," www.abmc.gov/abmc46.htm (accessed April 15, 2004).

Asante, Molefi Kete, ed. *Socio-Cultural Conflict Between African Americans and Korean Americans.* Lanham, MD: University Press of America, 2000.

Danico, Mary Yu. *The 1.5 Generation: Becoming Korean American in Hawaii.* Honolulu: University of Hawai'i Press, 2004.

Hurh, Won Moo. *Korean Immigrants in America: A Structural Analysis of Ethnic Confinement and Adhesive Adaptation.* Rutherford, NJ: Fairleigh Dickinson University Press, 1984.

Joyce, Patrick D. *No Fire Next Time: Black-Korean Conflicts and the Future of America's Cities.* Ithaca, NY: Cornell University Press, 2003.

Keller, Nora Okja. *Fox Girl.* New York: Penguin, 2002.

Kibria, Nazli. *Becoming Asian American: Second-Generation Chinese and Korean Identities.* Baltimore: Johns Hopkins University Press, 2002.

Kim, Kwang Chung, ed. *Koreans in the Hood: Conflict with African Americans*. Baltimore: Johns Hopkins University Press, 1999.

Lee, Jennifer. *Civility in the City: Blacks, Jews, and Koreans in Urban America*. Cambridge, MA: Harvard University Press, 2002.

National Association of Korean Americans, "History," www.naka.org (accessed April 15, 2004).

Yuh, Ji-Yeon. *Beyond the Shadow of Camptown: Korean Military Brides in America*. New York: New York University Press, 2002.

10

Rita Ciresi, *Sometimes I Dream in Italian* (2000)

PLOT SYNOPSIS

This novel, divided into two sections, details experiences from Angel Lupo's childhood and catalogues events from her adult life. It is a bildungsroman charting the life of an Italian American girl who lives in New Haven, Connecticut, with her parents and her older sister. *Sometimes I Dream in Italian* focuses primarily on Angel's relationship with her mother from whom Angel is to learn her Italian identity. While Angel respects her mother in many ways, she finds herself resisting her mother's instruction as she tries to forge her own identity in the ever-evolving U.S. cultural landscape.

When *Sometimes I Dream in Italian* opens in the first section, Angel is accompanying her mother Filomena on her weekly shopping trip to the butcher. The nine-year-old Angel is charged with scrutinizing Mr. Ribalta's every move, to make sure that he does not cheat the Lupos by either adding weight to the scales or doubling the wax paper. From this practice, Angel is to learn how to become an efficient wife and mother and follow in Filomena's footsteps. However, Angel is embarrassed by her mother's somewhat condescending attitude toward Mr. Ribalta. Though Filomena has patronized this butcher for years, she still does not trust him. After carefully inspecting each cut of meet she intends to purchase and ensuring that Mr. Ribalta wrap it properly, Filomena then engages in her weekly haggling exercise over the scraps. Though Mr. Ribalta knows that the Lupos have no dog, he pretends that he thinks they do so that Filomena's purchase of the scraps is less dehumanizing. In actuality, Filomena, who prides herself on her Italian thrift and old-fashioned common sense, does not care what Mr. Ribalta believes or pretends to believe. For her, the goal is to purchase as much as possible for as little as possible and to instill in Angel the value of bargaining and negotiation.

Just as Angel tries to reject much of what her mother tries to teach her, she also spends the greater portion of her childhood rejecting her father, referred to as Babbo. Embarrassed by his blue-collar occupation (a soda truck driver for a bottling company) and sickened by the smelly feet he exposes every evening upon returning home from work, Angel, along with older sister Lina, longs to believe that her father really lives a secretive and more exotic life. For if he has somehow escaped, if only temporarily, this mundane existence, then the Lupo girls could hope for a better life, too. Spying among his personal possessions, the two girls find a photograph of a young woman they decide must be their father's paramour. Excited that he may, in fact, be leading a double (and thus romantic) life, Angel and Lina search out this mysterious woman whenever they venture beyond the confines of the house. After a while, they tire of the game and focus on their own lives once again. Years later, after Babbo's death, when they are cleaning out their parents' house, the girls see the photograph again and realize that it is a younger Filomena. The "girlfriend" was their mother all along, the only woman for whom Babbo ever had any love. Even though the girls knew that their parents' relationship was far from perfect, they come to realize that their mother and father honored their commitment and provided a stable life for their daughters. The very life that Angel and Lina often reject is completely embedded in their identities and in their reality, but it will take years for them to realize the extent of this familial and ethnic connection.

When Angel is 10, she and Lina try to convince Filomena and Babbo (whose real name is Carlino) to adopt "American" names, Phyllis and Charles. Then the whole family, according to the girls, can become the Wolfs ("Lupo" in Italian means "wolf"). When their mother and father reject this idea, the two girls take matters into their own hands. In a symbolic gesture, they pilfer a photograph of their father and have a fake driver's license made up for him with the name Charles Wolf, which they carefully place in his wallet under his authentic license. Their goal is simply to use the fake license as a kind of talisman that will magically transform Carlino Lupo into Charles Wolf. Unfortunately, on one night when he is stopped for speeding, the officer on duty discovers both licenses and arrests Babbo until the matter can be resolved. Babbo spends a night in jail because of his daughters' prank, and Filomena must hire a lawyer to clear up the mess, an unnecessary expense, especially for someone of Filomena's financial thrift. Angel and Lina's attempt to detach themselves from their Italian heritage has cost the family, both literally and figuratively, as this peccadillo takes a toll on the family unit.

At the same time that the Lupos' lives are often filled with tension, there are times when they band together and share positive moments. On one such occasion the family joins a church outing on a bus trip to New York City to visit the Statue of Liberty. On the way there, Angel and Lina are once again embarrassed by their mother's behavior (Filomena makes a big fuss about where everyone must sit, and she constantly scolds the bus driver). The girls fear that this will be another horror story to add to many other childhood traumas. By journey's end, however, after they have visited the Statue of Liberty, with the girls actually making it all the way to the top, both Filomena and Babbo seem mellow and quite appreciative of their circumstances. In revisiting the Statue of Liberty, they are reminded of that day years ago when they first arrived in the harbor from Italy, with all of their hopes and dreams before them. Now, several years later, with their daughters in tow, they are reminded of their youthful and seemingly more carefree days. Both Filomena and Babbo express their love for Angel and Lina more openly and sincerely. It seems that they are reminded of the fact that part of their dreams came true, in the form of two healthy children. Angel and Lina feel the warmth of their parents' love on this day.

This equilibrium is short-lived when a few weeks later Filomena's mother, known as Nonna, dies. This loss affects Lina the most because she spent most of her free time next door at Nonna's house. For Lina, Nonna's house represented a refuge from Filomena's exacting ways. While at Nonna's house, Lina was encouraged to sharpen her creative skills, particularly in music; and Nonna always had special treats for her. Even though Filomena thought Nonna spoiled Lina and fueled an already overactive imagination, Lina was still allowed to spend time with her favorite grandmother. After Nonna's death Lina fears that she has lost the best friend she ever knew, and she feels that her life is now circumscribed far more than it ever was before. From this point on Lina will feel caged in and defeated, unlike her free-spirited Aunt Patty (or Pasquelina), for whom she is named and with whom she is reunited upon Nonna's death. Even though Aunt Patty tries to replace Nonna as Lina's mentor, Lina believes she will never escape the destiny of a mundane and unfulfilled life. It is during this time, as well, that Lina blossoms into a woman and becomes more detached from Angel, who has yet to enter puberty.

By the time Angel enters high school, both she and Lina must attend public school. When Babbo is laid off from his delivery job, he can no longer afford to pay the tuition to the private Catholic school. In high school, Angel and Lina get their first dose of racial conflict. With its predominantly black student population, the public high school is a far cry from the structured, uniform-required environment to which Angel and Lina have become accustomed. Soon after arriving, Angel and Lina have their first racial brawl during a physical education class. As punishment, they and the other girls are ordered to clean the women's bathroom. Instead of doing this job, however, Angel, Lina, and the black girls proceed to smoke marijuana and get to know each other better. Unorthodox though this bonding session is, the girls attempt to connect beyond the barriers of race. Though they will not become the best of friends, at the very least, they have learned to be civil. This segment concludes the first section of the novel.

In the second section, Angel and Lina are now adults. Angel is a single woman living in Poughkeepsie, New York, and writing for a greeting card company, while Lina is the married mother of two who lives in the suburbs of New Haven. Angel makes the requisite trips back to New Haven for her parents' birthdays and for various holidays. On one such occasion, she learns that a professor from Yale, a black woman, is conducting research on the now aged Italian American women who once worked at the local factory that manufactured women's purses. Known as the Pockabookie Ladies, these women, with their Sicilian accents, sleeveless multicolored muumuus, and black crocheted sweaters, represented everything that Angel and Lina wished to avoid. Though Filomena never worked at the factory, the girls thought that she suffered from Pockabookie-ism, and they were often embarrassed by her appearance. On another trip home, Angel must accompany Lina and Filomena to the market, when she takes stock yet again of her mother's decidedly Pockabookie look. For them, being Italian meant being a Pockabookie, a fate worse than death. On the drive to the market, Filomena comments on the negative changes suffered by the neighborhood, mainly because more blacks have moved there. Both Angel and Lina despise what they believe to be their mother's racist beliefs. Angel is especially perturbed when she notices her mother's reaction to Lina's renewing an acquaintance with a former high school classmate, a black male. Angel is reminded once again how she does not want to become her mother.

When Filomena suffers a stroke and must be hospitalized indefinitely, Angel finds herself missing the mother she so often ridiculed. She especially misses the weekly letters Filomena always wrote to her, including within obituaries from various friends or relatives whom Angel barely remembered. Before Filomena's stroke, Angel took these letters for granted; she thought her mother would always be present to criticize and harass her. Now, however, Angel is left with Filomena only in memories; for when she visits her mother in the nursing home, Filomena does not respond. Angel's relationship with Babbo has not improved over the years; they have hardly anything to say to each other during her monthly visits. This phase of Angel's life is fraught with sadness, not only over her mother's condition, but also over Lina's troubled marriage. Because Angel longs for the successful husband and the two precious children, she cannot understand why Lina is not happy. Phil is the perfect, caring husband who has provided Lina with every creature comfort. Still, Lina divulges to Angel that she is having an affair. Pained about Filomena and feeling inadequate and insecure in her own life, Angel thinks that neither she nor Lina has become the woman Filomena raised her to be. Though she never wanted to emulate Filomena before, Angel finds herself now echoing some of Filomena's expressions and kernels of wisdom.

As she approaches 30, Angel feels even more compelled to find a suitable mate. After spending years lusting after her brother-in-law, Angel seeks help by responding to a personal ad. When Dirk Diederhoff replies to her letter, Angel begins a new adventure. A bit arrogant and somewhat emotionally detached, Dirk is a German professor at Angel's alma mater, Vassar. The two of them date for several weeks, during which time Angel is determined to make the relationship work, even though every time they make love, Angel fantasizes about her muscular landlord. When Dirk proposes to Angel during their three-week vacation to Italy, she is prepared to accept. However, she soon realizes that Dirk is not the man for her because she lacks passion for him. Haunted as well by Lina's increasingly troubled marriage, the memory of her parents' strained relationship, and Babbo's rapidly deteriorating condition (Filomena has passed away by now), Angel does not want to make a mistake she will regret for the rest of her life. This emotional tension compels her to end the relationship and to forego, at least for the near future, matrimony and a family of her own.

Soon after Angel and Dirk terminate their relationship, Lina attempts suicide, and Angel is called to New Haven to help Phil care for
the children. Because Lina tried to kill herself by exposure to carbon
monoxide from the gas oven, Phil, in his very matter-of-fact and practical way, has the oven removed and replaced with an electric one, as
though a different oven will prevent Lina from attempting suicide
again. Though Phil cannot understand why his wife would want to kill
herself, Angel does understand Lina's frustrations somewhat, though
she is hesitant to explain them to Phil, since one of Lina's frustrations
is her disenchantment with her husband. In addition, Lina is no
longer thrilled with motherhood. The tony neighborhood where they
live feels more like a prison to Lina because she has nothing in common with the other housewives there. Women who sport frosted hair,
painted nails, and split skirts are no match for Lina's more creative nature. Phil, on the other hand, is content existing in this very mainstream world. Many months before, when he considers joining the
Rotary Club, Lina warns, in what seems a mere joke at the time: "Let
me know when you do, and I'll go stick my head in the oven" (Ciresi,
Sometimes I Dream in Italian, 128). Angel cannot bear to divulge to
Phil that the very life he has created for Lina has, in fact, trapped her.
Ironically, of course, Lina's situation vindicates Angel and her decision
to sever ties with Dirk. Rather than risk the possibility of being in an
unhappy relationship and with children no less, Angel would rather
continue her solo life. Interestingly enough, when she explains her decision to Phil, he admits that Angel has made the right choice.

By the novel's end, Lina appears to be on the road to recovery. She
asks Angel to drive her to the salon, in an effort to initiate positive
change. Lina even seems more aware of herself than others might give
her credit. She engages Angel is a heartfelt discussion about feelings,
aspirations, and frustrations. Though their lives are not the perfect
ones they imagined for themselves, at the very least Angel and Lina
have each other. While Angel envies Lina's "model" domestic life and
Lina envies Angel's freedom, the two may come to realize that their
ultimate happiness must emanate from inside and not from the acqui-
sitions or accomplishments they think they need to validate themselves. For now, each must take life one day at a time.

HISTORICAL BACKGROUND

Published in 2000, *Sometimes I Dream in Italian* is set during the
20-year period from 1970 to 1990, beginning when Angel is nine

years old and ending as she approaches 30. By this time, the New Haven, Connecticut, setting has a well-established Italian community, the result of early twentieth century east coast immigration patterns. When Italians began migrating to the United States in the latter half of the nineteenth century, mainly from southern Italy, they settled in great numbers in the New York City area. This trend continued into the early part of the twentieth century, well into the 1920s. Italians also began to venture out to other regions in the Hudson River Valley, namely Poughkeepsie and other points north and east into Connecticut. In *Sometimes I Dream in Italian,* Ciresi practically scripts this journey when she has Angel travel back and forth from her new home in Poughkeepsie, New York to her native home of New Haven, Connecticut. In this way, the novel honors the history of Italian settlement in this region.

Angel and Lina are the first in their family to be born in the United States, their parents having come to the country as mere youngsters with their parents. The elder Lupos, Babbo and Filomena, have a longtime emotional investment in the United States, as is clearly revealed when they visit the Statue of Liberty and recount for their daughters that day long ago when they first came to the United States. They speak with pride of the hard work and sacrifice their families made to ensure that they would have a better life.

Babbo and Filomena feel a sense of ownership over their Italian community. In their estimation, they have done well by fulfilling their families' wishes of working diligently to ensure an independent and morally sound life. And they want nothing less for their daughters. Products of the 1940s and 1950s, Filomena and Babbo define their progress by the protection of certain values. They believe that their neighborhood should remain the same as it has always been since they moved there. By the time they have school-age children, however, the neighborhood is changing. By the late 1960s, blacks have begun to move in, much to the horror of both of them. On one occasion, Filomena, speaking of the seven-member family who has moved in next door, states that they have come from "Lord knows where" (105). Even though they are immigrants like she once was, Filomena despises the dark skin of her Haitian neighbors. Angel even mocks her mother when she says that God must know where Haiti is even if Filomena does not. And if God knows where it is, then he must have created it and the people there just as he created the Lupos.

Angel and Lina, products of the 1960s and 1970s, have had more direct contact with blacks, given the migratory patterns of blacks to formerly all-white neighborhoods during this period. Moreover, Lina and Angel recognize greater similarity with the young blacks they meet, shared circumstances that neither Filomena nor Babbo would ever admit. When Angel and Lina are forced to leave the private Catholic school and transfer to the public school upon Babbo's dismissal from work, they recognize (even if they do not fully articulate the reality) the fact that their economic situation is now similar to that of the black students. They cannot afford to see themselves as superior to the black girls because economically they are no better than these girls. As easily as Angel and Lina might want to refer to the black girls by a racial epithet, these girls might just as easily refer to them as "guineas," a term mentioned throughout the novel, in part as a reminder to Angel and Lina of their tenuous circumstance and also in part as a reminder to the reader that any group is haunted by the hurtful rhetoric potentially spewed by another group.

The novel, to a great degree, traces the history of race relations in the United States, in this case, of course, a history represented by the conflict between Italian Americans and African Americans. In the late 1970s, when Angel and Lina are in high school, they become inured to the presence of black people, with both of them even befriending some black students. Lina and Angel come of age during a time when young people questioned authority and challenged all rules and moral codes. Especially for young white people, who recognized the hypocrisy of a society that prided itself on moral rectitude at the same time that it sanctioned race separation, subverting all rules seemed at the very least an exercise in consistency. So when Lina smokes marijuana and snorts cocaine not just with black students, but with black male students, she is rejecting all forms of societal control. Her behavior is, indeed, consistent with the trends of the iconoclastic 1970s. While Lina's behavior was certainly self-destructive, her cross-racial and cross-cultural interactions prepared her for an adult world that would be far different from her childhood.

By the late 1980s, when Lina and Angel are full-fledged adults and Lina is the mother of two, the racial strife that they faced as children is less pronounced in the lives of Lina's children. During one conversation with Angel, Lina states in a rather matter-of-fact tone that her little daughter Pammy has two black girls in her class. What would have been shocking to Babbo and Filomena a while back is of no concern to Lina. Moreover, the more inclusive world that Pammy is growing up in has made her more receptive to others. In one instance, Pammy tells Lina that Nicole and Daniella, the two black girls, are different, and when Lina is just about to unleash a minilecture on inclusion and race sensitivity, Pammy informs her mother that the girls are different because they wear beads in their hair. Granted, Pammy is still a naive child, and her innocent response is linked in large measure to her naivete. However, her response, too, offers hope for the new world that she now inhabits and will inhabit with the rapid elapse of time. To be sure, Pammy will meet with the evils of race prejudice in due course, but at the very least, her response reveals promise for a future less obsessed with race than it was in the past. With the early 1990s end to this 2000 novel, the reader, with a decade-long vantage, knows that the wheels of race inclusion and sensitivity move ever so slowly. Still, the novel challenges the reader to make the twenty-first century much better than the twentieth century.

LITERARY ANALYSIS

Race is addressed in the novel both directly and indirectly. Its more subtle emergence is presented via the relationship between mother and daughters, especially between Filomena and Angel. From the very beginning of *Sometimes I Dream in Italian,* Angel gets a lesson in race dynamics. The opening chapter finds Angel and her mother conducting their weekly shopping trip to the butcher, an otherwise innocent outing. However, race politics, as ever present in the U.S. cultural landscape, figure quite significantly also during the Lupos' exchange with Mr. Ribalta. For some time now Angel has wanted Filomena to purchase a chunk of Swiss cheese, only to be told, "I don't pay good money for holes" (3). To appease Angel, Mr. Ribalta gives the nine-year-old a slice of the cheese and teasingly calls her "Swiss Girl." In this gesture, pregnant with meaning, Mr. Ribalta offers Angel the possibility of seeing the world more broadly, beyond the circumscribed world of her Italian American neighborhood. In bestowing upon her a different nationality (or ethnicity), Mr. Ribalta invites Angel to think broadly about her identity and her place in the larger world.

In short, Mr. Ribalta is fighting against Filomena's desire to cultivate only an Italian identity that suppresses all outside influences. Filomena (along with Babbo) sees her Italian identity as the norm, a position from which all other ethnicities are made the other. Mr. Ribalta, however, would have Angel collapse the ethnic boundaries that serve only to separate people and make them fear each other. Angel, who can be both Swiss and Italian, will not be as regressive in her social views if she learns at this young age to embrace people over mere labels. That Mr. Ribalta's gesture has had a positive effect on Angel is evident when she states about the cheese: "I wanted to take a chunk of it home and slip it between a wedge of sharp pepperoni and a slice of salty prosciutto on a seeded roll" (3). Just as she wants to embed the Swiss cheese within the Italian foods, Angel is willing to cultivate another ethnicity within her Italian cultural being, instead of treating any non-Italian identity as a foreign entity or concept.

This opening scene provides the metaphor for considering race relations in the novel: Angel's relationship with Filomena becomes the tool by which the reader measures Angel's progressive development. When she rejects her mother's (and father's) increasingly antiquated notions of race, Angel becomes better equipped to function in what is already an apparently multicultural and multiethnic U.S. society. Both Filomena and Babbo, given their generational influences, maintain very narrow views of what being an American is. Without question, they see themselves as fully American, no matter their first-generation immigrant status. Even when Lina and Angel plead with them to adopt more "American-sounding" names (simply because the girls want greater peer acceptance in school), Filomena and Babbo reject the idea because they have already declared themselves complete Americans. Their white skin (though Babbo's is more olive than Filomena's) makes them American. Moreover, they refuse to alter their names because they do not want to risk having any "Negro-sounding" names. For them, the Italian names retain their white (hence, American) identities. Angel and Lina, on the other hand, have no concerns about being linked to other Americans, regardless of their ethnic origins.

Of course, Filomena and Babbo, believing themselves to be superior to all persons darker than they (Babbo bemoans America's ruination by Japanese and blacks), would never want to be compared to black people at any time or under any circumstance. However, Angel and Lina almost force Filomena to acknowledge a similarity during a trip to the market after the daughters become adults. While at the market, Lina encounters a former high school classmate, who greets her by saying, "What's happening?" Later, when everyone has returned to the car, Filomena asks her daughters why black people always greet each other with that particular expression. They then ask her why Italians greet each other with *che si dice,* and they also ask her what the expression means. When Filomena offers no suitable answers (stating only "Why do I have to know what everything *means* all the time? Why do I have to think?"), the girls' point is made. Every cultural group devises its own language, or dialect, or idiom. When one acknowledges such innovation across ethnic lines, one (if he or she is rational) must declare that no one group is superior to another. If they are similar, one cannot be superior to another. Later, when Angel learns that *che si dice* means "How's it going?" (119), an almost verbatim translation of "what's happening," she feels completely vindicated in her exchange with Filomena. Her point that Italians are not really different from, thus no better than, blacks is confirmed.

One reason that Angel and Lina are more sensitive to racial issues is that they have experienced minority status in their high school. With a two to one ratio of black to Italian, Roger Sherman High School provides the ideal sociological laboratory for the Lupo sisters to study race relations. Because blacks outnumber the Italian students, they exact a certain amount of social power over the Italians. No longer enjoying the majority position they have in their neighborhood, Lina and Angel now fully appreciate the strategies minorities must adopt simply to survive. The girls try to remain almost invisible so as not to offend the black students. In this microcosm, they learn that race always figures into cross-racial exchanges.

On one occasion, during one of the girls' physical education classes, the prominence of race is made abundantly clear. The teacher groups the class into teams for practice basketball games, careful to ensure racial parity to the extent that the aforementioned ratio will allow. Soon after the game begins, however, the teammates regroup themselves along racial lines, so that formerly opposing members are now playing for each other. The game suddenly ends in a brawl, with one classmate sustaining a minor injury. Lina and Angel find themselves, along with two black girls, being punished for the incident. The four are made to clean one of the bathrooms. Initially hostile toward Angel and Lina, Felicia and Terry ultimately sit down and chat with the Lupo sisters after Lina proves to them that she will not be intimidated. The girls find common ground in ridiculing the administration and in criticizing one of its recent attempts to "solve" the race problem at school. School officials hired two consultants, one black and one white, to conduct sensitivity workshops for the students that failed miserably. Felicia, Terry, Angel, and Lina all agree that the consultants were so naive in their attempt to convince the students that a colorblind posture provided the ideal way for addressing race. These girls realize that one cannot ignore ethnic and racial difference; instead one must acknowledge it and cope with it willingly and deliberately. Lina and Angel come to understand, unlike Filomena and Babbo, that they cannot simply ignore those who differ from them. Felicia and Terry are as American as Angel and Lina. While the four girls will never become close friends, at least they have been honest in their dialogue, or as honest as teenage posturing will allow.

That Lina and Angel had such a dialogue is so important in creating their racial awareness. Years later, when Lina is objectified by her extra-marital paramour Bob, she recognizes his narrow-minded perspective even though she has become too enervated by her personal life to cope very well. When Bob requests that she speak Italian phrases to him in the throes of passion, Lina realizes that she is no more to him than some exotic trinket. Her Italian-ness has not fully protected her whiteness in the way that her parents would have her believe. Race, for both Angel and Lina, is far more complex than mere white versus black. That they would want to embrace and acknowledge all ethnicities is understandable because they know that a mere reduction of race to black and white in the United States does not necessarily protect them. One might enjoy the majority position in one moment, only to be reduced to second-class citizenship in the next. Angel can and should embrace the Italian, the Swiss, the German represented by Dirk, and any other ethnic formation that makes her whole. That Lina's very "white" suburban existence is killing her, literally and figuratively, is further testament to the importance of such inclusion.

BIBLIOGRAPHY

Alba, Richard D. *Italian Americans: Into the Twilight of Ethnicity.* Englewood Cliffs, NJ: Prentice-Hall, 1985.

Ciresi, Rita. *Sometimes I Dream in Italian.* New York: Random House, 2000.

Cohen, Miriam. *Workshop to Office: Two Generations of Italian Women in New York City, 1900–1950.* Ithaca, NY: Cornell University Press, 1993.

Cosco, Joseph P. *Imagining Italians: The Clash of Romance and Race in American Perceptions, 1880–1910.* Albany: State University of New York Press, 2003.

Guglielmo, Jennifer, and Salvatore Salerno, eds. *Are Italians White? How Race is Made in America.* New York: Routledge, 2003.

Lipsitz, George. *The Possessive Investment in Whiteness.* Philadelphia: Temple University Press, 1998.

Richards, David A. J. *Italian American: The Racializing of an Ethnic Identity.* New York: New York University Press, 1999.

11

Chaim Potok, *The Chosen* (1967)

PLOT SYNOPSIS

The Chosen tells the story of two teenage Jewish American boys, Reuven Malter and Danny Saunders, who learn the value of friendship despite certain intrafaith and intracultural differences. The 15-year-olds first encounter each other in the early 1940s when they, playing for their respective school baseball teams, face off in a community rival game. The contest between the two teams entails more than a mere competition between opponents; it involves the rather bitter conflict between two sects of the Jewish faith. Narrated in the first person by Reuven, *The Chosen* details how Danny's team's deep Hasidic faith causes team members to view Reuven's team's less strict observance of Jewish religion as being indicative of flawed character. Therefore, a mere sports competition ultimately devolves into a moral and ethical battle. As Reuven intimates, "The fun and excitement was out of it now. Somehow the yeshiva team had translated this afternoon's baseball game into a conflict between what they regarded as their righteousness and our sinfulness" (Potok, *The Chosen*, 24).

In the novel's first chapter, Reuven and Danny find themselves facing each other not only in a battle of sportsmanship, but also in a battle of wit. Each tries to intimidate the other during one inning when Reuven is pitching to Danny. Both are key players for their teams, and this particular play is crucial to each team's potential victory. Staring each other down and determined to outperform and outwit the other, Reuven and Danny declare an almost personal war. After two strikes and one ball, the next play is significant. Danny, determined not to be humiliated by what he considers a physically and morally inferior team, hits the ball with such force that it strikes Reuven in the face, shattering his glasses and injuring his left eye. Reuven's team loses by one point, and the defeated boy is rushed to the hospital by his coach. Thus begins the unlikely relationship of Danny and Reuven.

In the hospital Reuven undergoes surgery on his eye. He befriends his two roommates, a young blind boy Billy Merrit and the adult Tony Savo, a former boxer. Both patients help Reuven to pass the time as he recovers from his operation. He must wait for a few days to see whether or not any permanent damage has been done. Reuven's father, a high school teacher and scholar, is very concerned about his son's prognosis. He visits Reuven daily and tries to impress upon his son the importance of controlling his anger at Danny. Because Reuven believes that Danny deliberately struck him, he finds difficulty in forgiving the boy's actions. Because Mr. Malter's health is already compromised, Reuven blames Danny for causing his father additional pain. As Reuven begins to recover, however, and as he experiences compassion for his roommates, whose circumstances are far more precarious than his, his anger subsides somewhat, and he begins to focus on other matters. Reuven marvels at how young Billy, plagued with total blindness, is so pleasant and engaging. Reuven promises both Billy and Billy's father Roger that he will call and visit after he and Billy are released. With this, Reuven is encouraged to focus on possibilities rather than disappointments. With the radio that Mr. Malter supplies him, Reuven stays abreast of increased U.S. involvement in World War II. The conflict abroad and the resultant loss of life make Reuven's condition pale in comparison.

Reuven's positive outlook is temporarily thwarted, however, when Danny Saunders appears one day in the hospital. Miffed that Danny has the audacity to present himself, Reuven expresses both anger and disgust at Danny. Refusing to accept his apology, Reuven belittles Danny, curses him, and makes him feel even worse for his actions during the game. Realizing that he will make no inroad with Reuven on this day, Danny departs feeling frustrated and somewhat demoralized. Later, when Mr. Malter visits his son and Reuven divulges what happened, Mr. Malter scolds his son for his behavior, admonishing him to accept the apology and to listen to whatever Danny has to share.

On the next day, undaunted yet again, Danny returns, this time refusing to be swayed by Reuven's anger. Reuven, however, receives Danny cordially, and the two engage in a meaningful conversation, not only about the game and Danny's remorse about it, but also about the actual feelings Danny experienced on the day of the game (the hatred he felt for Reuven and his team). Danny is now determined to come to terms with those feelings, and he wants to continue a dialogue with Reuven so that they can better understand their intrafaith differences. A Hasidic Jew, whose conservative black attire and side curls distinguish him from others, Danny is being groomed to assume his father's place as rabbi one day. Rabbi Isaac Saunders, a self-righteous man determined to instill in his son strict adherence to Talmudic law, brooks no disobedience from Danny. Now struggling with his own commitment to the conservative faith, Danny questions the extent to which the faith led him to harbor such animosity toward Reuven during the game. Admitting that he wanted actually to kill Reuven, Danny now needs to analyze that impulse. He requires open and honest dialogue with his nemesis/friend. Reuven, whose father encourages analysis and interrogation and the free exchange of ideas, is poised for such conversation.

Each boy does have something to offer the other. Their lives are both similar and different. Reuven, whose father wants him to be a mathematician and university teacher, wants instead to be a rabbi. Danny, whose father wants him to be a rabbi, would rather be a psychologist. On the other hand, Reuven has a father who listens to him and encourages father-son dialogue, while Danny's father adheres to very strict codes of child-rearing. He practices silence with Danny, engaging in "conversation" only when the two are studying the Talmud together. Danny needs someone with whom he can share ideas in an honest and trustworthy fashion. When Reuven tells his father that he thinks he and Danny will become friends, Mr. Malter is pleased. He encourages Reuven to make Danny his true friend, reminding Reuven that each person requires the company of at least two other persons in life: a teacher and a friend.

When Danny returns for another visit, Reuven finally understands why his father has prodded him to become Danny's friend. Mr. Malter is already present, and Reuven discovers that Danny and Mr. Malter already know each other, though Danny did not know until now that Mr. Malter is, in fact, Reuven's father. Some weeks before, Danny happened upon Mr. Malter in the library, and he asked the stranger to suggest to him some books to read. Danny, a very bright boy, desires knowledge beyond only religious texts. Mr. Malter and Danny have been conversing about intellectual ideas and about the suggested readings for quite a while. Even though Mr. Malter has known that

Danny's father would disapprove of Danny's broad reading tastes, he justifies his involvement by arguing that if Danny is going to read outside the prescribed Jewish canon anyway, he ought to have some authoritative guidance. Once Danny and Reuven survive their initial shock about Danny's past interaction with Mr. Malter, they agree to develop their friendship once Reuven is released from the hospital. Mr. Malter is very pleased that two obviously bright and fairly strong-willed young men have found each other. They have in each other channels through which to express their intellectual energies.

The softball game that resulted in Reuven's injury was held on a Sunday. Reuven is released from the hospital on the following Friday, and on Saturday he accompanies Danny to Rabbi Saunders's synagogue for evening services so that the rabbi can assess Reuven's suitability to be Danny's friend. Finding Danny's father to be both detached and kind, Reuven is still confirmed in his belief that Rabbi Saunders is somewhat of a tyrant. That a father would not engage in friendly conversation with his elder son (Danny has a younger brother and a younger sister), Reuven finds appalling. Nevertheless, Reuven suffers through his interview/test for Danny's sake. While attending service, Reuven learns of the weekly ritual that Rabbi Saunders foists upon Danny. During his lecture/sermon the rabbi deliberately punctuates his presentation with factual errors, after which he questions Danny on the accuracy of the lesson. That Danny would be subjected to this public spectacle is horrifying for Reuven. Disallowed, however, from sympathizing for very long with Danny, Reuven is also challenged by Rabbi Saunders with regard to the accuracy of the lecture. Initially dumbfounded, Reuven answers the rabbi's questions satisfactorily, proving his intellectual prowess and his worthiness of a friendship with Danny. After the service, Rabbi Saunders congratulates Reuven on his performance and thanks him for befriending Danny, all the while admitting, however, that he had his doubts about Danny's developing a friendship with the son of David Malter, a non-Hasidic Jew and one whose scholarly writings challenge the tenets that Rabbi Saunders holds so dear.

The following week Reuven returns to school and enjoys his "celebrity" status among his peers; he is now a hero for having been injured during a ball game. Reuven meets Danny after school at the library, and the two initiate what will be the beginning of many conversations about faith, Hasidim, and the intellectual life. Danny has begun to read more about Jewish history, and he is stunned to learn that not all historians report favorably on Hasidim. Now reading

Freud and deciding he must learn German, Danny is hungry for the kind of knowledge that will further challenge his religious beliefs. The following Saturday, Reuven joins Danny for a private teaching session with Rabbi Saunders. This day will mark a significant turning point in the lives of all concerned. During a few moments of privacy (while Danny is out of the room), Rabbi Saunders questions Reuven about the kind of reading Danny is doing at the library, revealing to Reuven that he has known about Danny's eclectic reading and about Danny's consultations with Reuven's father. Reuven is shocked to learn of Rabbi Saunders's knowledge. The rabbi pleads with Reuven to tell him all he knows, assuring Reuven that he will divulge nothing to Danny and that he is, in fact, pleased that at the very least, Danny has Reuven's father to guide him in his reading. Feeling trapped and traitorous, Reuven tells Rabbi Saunders everything.

After the session, while Danny is escorting Reuven part of the way home, Reuven divulges to Danny all that transpired with Danny's father. Though miffed that his father cannot talk to him, Danny is relieved to know that his father is aware of his reading and of his long-term friendship with Reuven's father. Reuven still does not understand why Rabbi Saunders cannot speak directly to his son. Later, Mr. Malter tries to explain to Reuven, after Reuven describes to him what has happened, that Rabbi Saunders is acting in the only way he knows how, given how he was raised and how he was taught to raise his son (with silence and detachment). Reuven then becomes the vessel through whom father and son communicate.

Reuven and Danny complete their school year and spend much time together throughout the summer, with Danny making considerable progress in his study of Freud and German. During the next school year, their friendship strengthens. The following summer, Reuven's father becomes very ill and must be hospitalized. During this time, Reuven moves in with the Saunders family and grows fond of them, even though he still has reservations about the way Rabbi Saunders treats Danny. In the fall, the two enter college together and support each other through this adjustment period. Reuven tackles symbolic logic, while Danny questions the psychology department's commitment to broad-based knowledge.

By the winter of 1947, the friendship between Danny and Reuven is plagued with its most challenging test. International efforts to establish a Jewish homeland to compensate Jewish survivors for what they had lost before and during World War II gain momentum. These "Zionist" activities David Malter supports with all of his waning energy. Rabbi Saunders, on the other hand, believes that a created Israeli state is a sacrilege and undermines the law of the Torah. Both men are absolute in their convictions. When the rabbi learns of Malter's "extreme" activities, he forbids Danny from having any more to do with the Malters. Reuven is heartbroken when he cannot even speak to Danny at college. For two years, Danny and Reuven are kept apart. During this time, David Malter intensifies his efforts in the interest of Israel. In the winter of 1947–48, he suffers a heart attack and is hospitalized for weeks. Still, Reuven is left to fend for himself. By the late spring of 1948, when Israel is established, Rabbi Saunders's anti-Zionist activities have lost momentum. Still, his ban against the Malters remains in effect for sometime thereafter. One day, Danny suddenly resumes his interaction with Reuven.

By the novel's end, Rabbi Saunders accepts Danny's decision not to enter the rabbinate. After he has made peace with his son's choice, he instructs his congregation to do likewise. Both Danny and Reuven graduate summa cum laude, with Danny planning to enter Columbia University in 1950 and Reuven spending the year studying for his smicha (rabbinic ordination). Both men vow to remain friends, knowing of course that their lives are changed forever.

HISTORICAL BACKGROUND

The Chosen is set in the Williamsburg section of Brooklyn, New York, during the mid- to late-1940s. This area is inhabited largely by Jewish citizens of various Hasidic sects, for whom the education of their children is the highest priority. Both Danny and Reuven, in large measure, benefit from this emphasis on education. The novel is contextualized not only by place and religion, but also by historical event. The evolution of World War II figures prominently as the backdrop for Reuven and Danny's emerging friendship. The "war" they declare on the baseball field symbolizes on American soil the important war being fought in Europe. War and conflict as historical concepts are located in *The Chosen* as thematic concepts as well.

By the time Danny and Reuven meet in the spring of 1944, the United States has been involved in World War II for over two years, having entered the conflict after Japan bombed Pearl Harbor on December 7, 1941. In the spring of 1944, the Allies (mainly Britain, the United States, and the Soviet Union) have begun to make great progress against the Axis powers (Germany, Italy, and Japan). When Allied forces storm Normandy, France (on what would be known as

D-Day), the end of the war is imminent, and the defeat of Hitler and his evil regime is soon to be realized within months, by mid-1945.

The peace established with the end of World War II echoes the emergent peace established between Reuven and Danny. Interestingly enough, just as World War II reaches its climax in 1944, Danny and Reuven have their greatest conflict. Even when Danny attempts to be-friend Reuven in those waning days in the spring of 1944, Reuven is distrustful of his baseball nemesis. Over the course of the next year, however, Danny and Reuven find common ground, even though Reuven is still leery of Rabbi Saunders and quite critical of his parental interaction with Danny (or lack thereof). Still, within weeks of the ac-cident that brought the two boys together, Rabbi Saunders makes Reuven his, albeit uneasy, ally when he asks Reuven about Danny's reading habits. Slowly, the Malter-Saunders conflict is eased (at least for a while). By the summer of 1945, a month before President Tru-man orders the bombing of Nagasaki and Hiroshima and officially brings an end to World War II, Reuven moves into the Saunders household while his father recuperates in the hospital from his first heart attack. Reuven has officially entered the sanctuary of his former enemy, and even though peace has been established, Reuven and Danny are still different people, representing different factions, Hasidic and non-Hasidic, much in the same way that the political/ international opponents fighting in World War II represent distinct factions.

The peace, by virtue of its newness, is fragile. Within a couple of years, Danny and Reuven will be forced again to be "political" oppo-nents when Rabbi Saunders takes issue with David Malter's endorse-ment of a Jewish state. The sons suffer the brunt of this conflict when old frictions and fractures are once again exposed. Similarly, the Soviet Union, the United States' ally in World War II, will emerge as a staunch enemy as the Cold War unfolds in the 1950s (the decade ap-proached at the end of the novel).

The Chosen, originally published in 1967, is in many ways influ-enced by events that occurred not only before World War II, but also in the interim years between the end of World War II and the latter 1960s. From the time the United Nations partitions the former Pales-tine state and officially creates Israel in 1948, major conflicts arise be-tween the Palestinians (and their Arab supporters) and the Israelis (Jews). Soon after Israel is established, the Arab-Israeli War of 1948–1949 ensues, with five Arab nations (Egypt, Transjordan, Syria, Lebanon, and Iraq) immediately attacking Israel. From 1948 on, many other conflicts occur, with Israel increasingly occupying territory beyond its official 1948 boundaries. In what is known as the Six-Day War of 1967, Israel expanded into the Golan Heights (formerly of Syria), into the West Bank (formerly of Jordan), and into the Gaza Strip (formerly of Egypt). Palestinians who had occupied the Israeli area before 1948 flee to surrounding countries, and even more flee the areas "occupied" by Israel in 1967. Tensions have remained constant throughout the second half of the twentieth century and now into the twenty-first century.

These historical tensions, like those in World War II, certainly inform the narrative tensions prevalent in *The Chosen*. While the World War II conflict contextualizes the Reuven-Danny war, the Arab-Israeli conflict mirrors, to some extent, the battle between Rabbi Saunders and David Malter. Though these two conflicts do not occur simultaneously (by the time Israel is officially established, Rabbi Saunders has rescinded his ban against the Malters), they are similar in regard to their intensity. Just as the Arabs and Israelis are violently committed to their beliefs regarding land occupation, Rabbi Saunders and David Malter are uncompromisingly devoted to their beliefs. Rabbi Saunders is willing to cause his son (and himself, in fact) emotional harm by intensifying his "unspoken" feud with Malter and the Zionists. So devoted to the cause of Zionism is David Malter that he risks his physical health in rallying help for the Israeli state. Ironically, David Malter has implied that Rabbi Saunders, while a learned and sincere man, is plagued by fanaticism. Yet Malter also becomes a fanatic when he commits himself to the partition effort. Though each man, in his estimation, has at heart the interest of the Jewish people, their intracultural conflict diminishes the very humanity they strive to protect. Unfortunately, history continues to showcase humankind's inhumanity to humankind.

LITERARY ANALYSIS

The Chosen details the pain caused by intracultural conflict and the prejudices harbored by two subcultural factions. The Hasidic perspective, represented by Rabbi Saunders, holds that non-Hasidic Jews are not as devoted to Jewish law and are thus inferior to Hasidim. Theirs is a conservative, fundamental view of the Talmud. Tradition must rule in the Hasidic world, with no latitude for interrogation or subversive analysis. Rabbi Saunders's yeshiva teaches in Yiddish in respect for tradition, while criticizing the less traditional schools for teaching in Hebrew. Believing Hebrew to be the Holy Word, the rabbi's group thinks it to be unspeakable to utter the language in a common school. As leader of his group and of his family, Rabbi Saunders expects unconditional loyalty from his flock. He prepares Danny to assume future rabbinic responsibility, and as the elder son, Danny is to accept these duties graciously and with serious intent. The non-Hasidic perspective, represented by David Malter, while respecting the more restrictive faction, believes in a more practical religion, one consistent with real-world changes and experiences. The non-Hasidim bemoan what they believe to be the fanaticism of the Hasidim. Malter questions any group that holds itself to be self-righteous and superior as though its religious perspective alone is the only truth.

This conflict is presented via the metaphor of blindness. The issue of blindness is broached early in the novel when Reuven's physical sight is threatened by the unfortunate baseball accident. Before and after his surgery, he faces the possibility that he may lose sight in his left eye. This battle between sightedness and blindness is compounded by the presence of Billy Merrit, Reuven's hospital mate who is completely blind. These tumultuous circumstances surrounding physical blindness and the possibility of blindness underscore the main questions posed throughout the novel: To what extent is physical sightedness a gift and to what extent is it a hindrance? How do people "see" (i.e., view, perceive) their world and their fellow man?

On the one hand, everyone in the novel would probably agree that sightedness is a gift and that anyone given a choice would opt for sight instead of blindness. However, physical sight ironically offers persons the "privilege" of bias when they so easily pass judgment on others by virtue of how they look or how they present themselves. Just as Reuven judges Danny because of his black clothes, his black hat, and his ear locks, the Hasidim judge the non-Hasidim for their lack of these accessories. Once each sees the other, barriers are erected, beliefs are established, and fears are made real. In this way, sightedness, in fact, becomes a hindrance from true human interaction and communication. Bias is made acceptable because of sight. The Hasidim and non-Hasidim alike seem to say, "I see you; you are different. We have no basis for communion."

On the other hand, when one observes the blind Billy Merrit, one finds him to be humane, kind, and receptive to all with whom he comes in contact. He is not gifted with the "privilege" of bias. He cannot pass judgment on people the moment he "sees" them. Instead, he must listen to people and "feel" their presence and their intent.

Though some might see Billy's world as restricted because he is blind, it is, in fact, broad and fraught with possibility. To Billy, every human being has the potential of being a friend. Moreover, Billy knows what true loss is; therefore, he does not take companionship for granted as do the sighted. He does not have the luxury of choosing friends by how they look. When one exists in a world where physical attributes truly do not matter, he is poised to receive and accept people on a higher set of principles. When one considers Billy's circumstance (sight stripped from an innocent child), human conflict is made all the more petty, especially such conflict between intracultural, intrareligious groups.

The issue of blindness is manipulated in the novel again when one more closely assesses Rabbi Saunders's blindness. Ironically, he expresses blind faith in his religion, evident even in his strict adherence to Talmudic principle. Opposed to the establishment of a Jewish state because imperfect mankind is creating it, he is willing to wait for the arrival of the Messiah before a Jewish land is founded. Yet he does not extend such blind faith to human beings who have shown him nothing but respect and gratitude. That he would forbid his son from further interaction with the only friend he has known and cause both Danny and Reuven undue emotional strain is indicative of a tyrannical strain that he justifies because it is grounded in this warped blind religious faith. Here blindness is both positive and negative again. That Rabbi Saunders is committed to religion is, of course, commendable; however, when this religion diminishes the very humanity that would make him an effective rabbi, then the blind faith is corrupted and distorted.

That sightedness can act as a disability is confirmed when Reuven finds himself puzzled by Danny's demeanor. Trying to explain Danny's persona to his father, Reuven declares: "The way he acts and talks doesn't seem to fit what he wears and the way he looks. It's like two different people" (75). Indeed, Danny is two different people: the one Reuven expected him to be and the one he really is. Reuven learns that he cannot define others one-dimensionally. Danny is a complex figure. Had Reuven never suffered the injury and had he simply passed Danny coincidentally on the street, he would have made assumptions that would never have been challenged. The ball's striking his head and his eye figuratively shocks him out of his comfort zone and forces him to crack the surface of the individual, rather than relying only on the surface to define the individual.

The novel teaches as its main lesson the necessity of human beings in finding a common bond, a common motivation. That shared desire will reveal other similarities previously unknown. The very reason that Reuven's team is playing Danny's team proves this point. The various Jewish parochial schools form baseball teams and community leagues to prove their American allegiance during World War II. In their role as devoted Americans, they find a shared space that has resulted in a solid bond between two young men whose friendship would have remained elusive. Having discovered each other, however, Reuven and Danny also find themselves personifying the very essence of true friendship. As Reuven's father explains, echoing a Greek philosopher, "...two people who are true friends are like two bodies with one soul" (74). That a Hasidic Jew and a non-Hasid would be described as sharing the same soul (given the belief of Hasidim that non-Hasidim were doomed to hell) forces one to consider and even embrace human interaction beyond established boundaries of prejudice and suspicion. David Malter also insists that "[h]onest differences of opinion should never be permitted to destroy a friendship" (219). Here, Mr. Malter allows persons to retain their individuality while at the same time remaining loyal to their role in the human family.

The novel's title is replete with meanings that underscore this denunciation of prejudice and separation. It is obvious that Danny is "chosen" by the circumstance of birth to assume the rabbinic role of his father. Yet Reuven has been "chosen" by his own inclination and desire to assume the rabbinic role. Both Danny and Reuven have been "chosen" to bring unity to the overall Jewish community and to remind this community that the Jewish are the "chosen" people, regardless of intersectional differences. As these two boys grow into young men, their maturity brings about a maturity in the communities they represent. Though sectional rivalries will continue to plague humanity (after all, human beings are still imperfect), at the very least, Reuven and Danny have offered a template for further advancement and liberation.

BIBLIOGRAPHY

American-Israeli Cooperative Enterprise, "Israel and the States," www.us-israel.org/jsource/History/parttoc.html (accessed May 10, 2004).
Brodkin, Karen. *How Jews Became White Folks and What That Says About Race in America*. New Brunswick, NJ: Rutgers University Press, 1998.

Fishman, Sylvia Barack. *Jewish Life and American Culture*. Albany: State University of New York Press, 2000.

Heilman, Samuel C., and Steven M. Cohen. *Cosmopolitans and Parochials: Modern Orthodox Jews in America*. Chicago: University of Chicago Press, 1989.

Jews Not Zionists Official Web site, "Current Issues," www.jewsnotzionists. org (accessed May 4, 2004).

Kugelmass, Jack, ed. *Between Two Worlds: Ethnographic Essays on American Jewry*. Ithaca, NY: Cornell University Press, 1988.

Philipson, Robert. *The Identity Question: Blacks and Jews in Europe and America*. Jackson: University Press of Mississippi, 2000.

Potok, Chaim. *The Chosen*. New York: Ballantine, 1967.

United Nations Official Web site, "Human Rights," www.un.org (accessed May 4, 2004).

12

Amy Wilentz, *Martyrs' Crossing* (2001)

PLOT SYNOPSIS

Set in the late 1990s, in the midst of the continued Israeli-Palestinian conflict, *Martyrs' Crossing* examines, from a deeply personal perspective, the political machinations that perpetuate the conflict. At the beginning of the novel, Marina Raad Hajimi, in an effort to secure medical attention for her two-year-old son Ibrahim, has walked from her home in Ramallah toward Jerusalem. Because the best hospital is located in Jerusalem, Marina hopes that she will have no difficulty crossing over the border into Israel. Unfortunately, two bus bombs were set off earlier in the day in Jerusalem, and all security checkpoints have been closed. But because Ibrahim's condition is worsening, Marina thinks that border authorities may take pity on her and allow her entry. As Marina approaches the Shuhada checkpoint, the crowd multiplies, while emotions intensify. Other Palestinians, angry about the closures and about being subjected to Israeli control at the borders, have amassed in the area, and they threaten civil unrest.

To quell the situation, the Shuhada commander, Israeli Lieutenant Ari Doron, orders the deployment of sound grenades and tear gas. With this deployment and with the approach of nightfall and a sudden storm, the crowd does disperse. However, Marina, given the urgency of her situation, retreats temporarily, only to return to seek passage. Walking back and forth in front of the guardhouse for quite a while (and in the pouring rain), Marina begs the soldiers to permit Ibrahim and her entry into Israel. They ignore her request, until finally an Arab bystander, Mahmoud Sheukhi, who has been observing the spectacle, confronts the soldiers and insists that they at least allow mother and child refuge in the guardhouse. Finally, Doron relents, but he will not permit Sheukhi to accompany them.

Once inside, Marina pleads her case even more. Ibrahim's breathing has become more irregular as his condition deteriorates. Doron places a call to authorities to ask permission to allow the woman and child passage. After being given the bureaucratic runaround, from one telephone call to the next, Doron is finally told to deny entry. However, concerned more for the sick child than for bureaucracy, Doron allows Marina and Ibrahim to take the ambulance that he had called for one of his injured men. When the emergency medical crew first spies Ibrahim, they realize the gravity of his condition, and they begin to work on him immediately. Unfortunately, their efforts are unsuccessful, and the child dies only minutes later.

Ibrahim's death threatens even more widespread political unrest. The Palestinians blame Israeli inhumanity for the child's death, while the Israeli government moves quickly to spin the details of the Shuhada incident in its favor. Making matters more volatile is the fact that Marina is the wife and daughter of two very important men on the Palestinian political front. Marina's husband Hassan Hajimi is currently sequestered in an Israeli prison for his alleged terrorist activities with the Hamas group. Known as an outspoken activist for the Arab (Palestinian) cause, Hassan has now lost his only child. That he will redouble his efforts against Israeli control is a possibility or perceived threat. Marina's father, Dr. George Raad, a Boston cardiologist and famous writer, has used his platform to defend the Palestinian people; his more recent writings have been critical of the Palestinian authorities who George believes have become more concerned with their own aggrandizement over true Palestinian liberation. George left his former Palestine homeland many years ago, but he still remained dedicated to the cause. When the novel opens, he is still in Boston, but upon the death of Ibrahim, he returns to the West Bank (to Ramallah) to support his daughter in her bereavement.

From the moment he arrives for his grandson's funeral, George must face the fact that the Palestinians fully intend to exploit Ibrahim's death. From his old friend and more recently his nemesis, Ahmed Amr, George learns that the Palestinian government intends to use the "martyred" Ibrahim to coerce the Israelis to resume negotiations. Fully intending to incite their own youth (Arab men) to protest in the streets and to cause a violent spectacle that will embar-

rass the Israelis before the international media, the Palestinian authorities will instigate a "Find the Soldier" campaign. This maneuver is designed to locate the unknown Israeli soldier, Ari Doron, whom the
Palestinians now blame for Ibrahim's death. George despises this ploy,
and he becomes even more disenchanted about the man Ahmed has
become: a politician instead of a committed activist.

At the same time that George is adjusting to these harsh truths
about life back on the West Bank, Ari Doron is confronted with his
own intranational political problems. Even though he ultimately de-
fied his superiors and authorized passage for Marina and Ibrahim,
Doron is still the target of much hatred across the border. To exacer-
bate problems for him, the Israeli authorities have insisted that he lie
about what actually transpired on the night of the incident.

Soon Doron finds himself facing Colonel Daniel Yizhar, an official
from the Israeli army on whom the Israeli government depends in
times of crisis. Yizhar is well-known for remedying problems by any
means necessary. In this circumstance, it is Yizhar's duty to persuade
Doron to accept the Israeli spin on Ibrahim's death. According to
Yizhar, the following really occurred: Doron was merely following
military procedure when he did not allow Marina and Ibrahim immediate passage, given the civil unrest following the bus bombings. He
did allow the mother and child into the guardhouse as a matter of
courtesy. As a precaution, he ran her name through the computer
whereupon he discovered that her husband was a prisoner of Israel.
Throughout this process, Ibrahim did not appear to be especially ill.
He then checked with his superiors, explained the child's predicament, and a few minutes later the ambulance arrived.

Of course, Doron knows that this version is inaccurate on three
major accounts. First, he did not allow the two immediate entrance
into the guardhouse. Mother and child spent a long time unprotected
by the rain and wind. Second, this version implies that the ambulance
was called expressly for Ibrahim, when in fact it was called for one of
Doron's slightly injured men. Third, Doron placed a special call on a
high-level security line to an unknown senior official who instructed
him not to permit the mother and child to pass into Israel. Still, of
course, Doron disobeys, albeit too late for Ibrahim.

Yizhar insists that his newly created version will be the official version, and he instructs Doron that he is not to speak to the media and
that he is not to reveal to anyone that he was the soldier in charge that
night. Sensing that Doron feels guilty about Ibrahim's death, Yizhar
reminds him that the security of Israel is more important than such a

useless emotion as guilt. Nevertheless, when Doron leaves Yizhar's office, he is as guilt-ridden and remorseful as he was before arriving there. He cannot shake the feeling that he should have ignored protocol minutes earlier and ushered Marina and Ibrahim into Israel much sooner.

In the meantime, Marina tries to adjust to life without Ibrahim and to life with her father back in Ramallah. Having lived on the West Bank now for four years, she and George are somewhat estranged. In an ironic twist, Marina blames her father to a degree for her predicament; she came to the West Bank from her comfortable U.S. home in part because of the nostalgic way her father always talked about his homeland and the Palestinian cause. She fell in love with an activist, married, and had Ibrahim. Her life changed completely. George, to some degree, blames Marina, whose recent loss has forced him back home to confront past demons that he is no longer physically able to combat. That they are brought together under these circumstances makes their relationship all the more strained. Having George's assistant Philip present helps to ease tensions a bit. Still father and daughter must interact with each other rather gingerly.

Doron, increasingly racked with guilt, disguises himself and slips away to Ramallah so that he can catch a glimpse of Marina. Drawn to her, not only because of her understated beauty, but also because of her noble strength, Doron is curious about how she is coping with this tragedy. Though it is certainly dangerous for him to be outside of Israel, especially with the "Find the Soldier" campaign gaining momentum, Doron disregards the potential threat and follows Marina about in the shadows.

While Doron spies on Marina, a reluctant George attends a meeting of Palestinian officials hosted by Ahmed. Torn between a still strong loyalty to his old friend and suspicion about Ahmed's current motives, George decides to give Ahmed the benefit of the doubt and to accept the invitation. Soon after arriving at Orient House (where the meeting is being held), George realizes, however, that Ahmed intends to operate only from a political motivation and not out of any sense of compassion for George's loss. After exploiting the sympathies of the men sitting around the table (regarding the death of an innocent child), Ahmed states that the Palestinian government will encourage the young men in the streets to continue protesting against the Israelis and to step up efforts in the "Find the Soldier" campaign. With no real regard to George's feelings about the matter, Ahmed bulldozes ahead, whereupon George rises unceremoniously and leaves without uttering a word to Ahmed.

On the following day, while George and Philip are having lunch in an East Jerusalem hotel, Mahmoud, Marina's advocate on the crucial night, approaches and asks if he might share with them his knowledge of the events leading up to Ibrahim's death. George insists on only an abbreviated version, at the end of which Mahmoud also supplies the name of Ari Doron, the infamous object of the "Find the Soldier" campaign. Insulted when George is rather dismissive of him and his information, Mahmoud insists that George must do something with this information, that he owes the Palestinian people to act on their behalf by bringing Doron to justice. Mahmoud then questions George's loyalty and courage, extending his doubts to Marina, whom Mahmoud also suspects of knowing Doron's name but not revealing it.

Both George and Marina, understanding the magnitude of their knowledge, are hesitant to share it with others, and especially with Hassan, for fear of what might happen. Were something untoward to happen to Doron, Hassan would be blamed, regardless of his actual culpability. Still, when George and Marina are asked to make an appearance at a rally organized by Palestinian students, they agree to do so. George despises the idea of being a pawn in Ahmed's political game, however. He decides, as a consequence to these feelings, to use the platform to state his true opinion about the political maneuvers and exploitation of his grandson's death. George states very passionately that the soldier in question did not kill Ibrahim, that instead those like Ahmed who have sold the Palestinian cause for political gain are really to blame. He insists that the current Israeli-Palestinian conflict is nothing more than a game, exercised now merely to advance the careers of officials on both sides.

In the middle of his speech, George is interrupted by chants, shouts, and applause; however, the response is not meant for him. Through the crowd word has spread that Hassan is to be freed. Ahmed, ever the politician and ever prepared, has already negotiated the release and planned the sudden leak of information. George is then upstaged by Ahmed, whose success in securing Hassan's release results in the redoubled support of the Palestinian people.

Mahmoud, who also attends the rally, is incensed that George does not seize the opportunity there to reveal Doron's name. He questions, in fact, why George not only rails against Ahmed and Palestinian officials, but also protects the identity of an Israeli soldier. Attributing George's action/inaction either to disloyalty or mental duress (given the tragedy), Mahmoud decides he must take matters into his own hands and seek justice.

The rally also serves as a lightning rod for Doron's now very strained relationship with Yizhar. Disguising himself once again, Doron attends the rally. Yizhar, however, spies him there on news footage supplied to Yizhar by his underlings. When Doron finally appears before Yizhar, the colonel is not surprisingly perturbed at the insolent lieutenant. Yizhar warns Doron that he must start acting in the best interest of Israel and that he must start by appearing on Army Radio for an interview that Yizhar has already scheduled, during which Doron is to reiterate the spin that Israeli officials have already put on the night in question. After a heated confrontation, Doron leaves Yizhar's office without committing to the interview. Yizhar now thinks he should have killed Doron when he had the chance.

After Hassan is released, George and Philip decide to move into a hotel so that Marina and Hassan can have privacy. Soon after the two men move into the American Colony Hotel, Doron pays George a visit. Having recently realized that it was Yizhar who gave him the order on the telephone not to allow Marina and Ibrahim into Israel, Doron is determined now to defy Yizhar. Doron hands over a gun to George and tells George to do with it whatever he would like, even if it means shooting Doron, who feels the need for penance of some kind. George does not oblige, but Doron insists that he keep the gun.

Doron then decides to pay a visit to Marina and ask her forgiveness, though he knows that Hassan is now there, too. By this point, Mahmoud (and his radical nephew Jibril) are stalking Doron. They follow him to the American Colony Hotel, and they follow him to the Hajimis' house. When Doron arrives at the Hajimis' house, Marina answers the door, clearly shocked to see Doron standing there. She pleads with him to leave before Hassan comes downstairs. After some urging, Doron finally relents. As he leaves, Hassan makes his approach but too late. By the time he rushes outside, he discovers only Doron's abandoned vehicle. Hassan realizes immediately that Doron has been kidnapped and that he will be blamed for it. Perturbed at Marina for protecting the soldier (Marina has come to realize that Doron, given the circumstances, did try to help her that night), Hassan knows he must go into hiding, as the Israelis will be looking for him.

Mahmoud and Jibril steal away with Doron, not knowing exactly what they will do with him. They inflict some physical abuse, but they ultimately release him. Mahmoud finally appreciates the fact that only tragedy will result for his family if he and Jibril were to kill Doron.

George, with Doron's gun in tow, goes in search of Ahmed, whom he discovers once condoned an assassination attempt on George's life.

Now very weak from his heart condition, George is practically incoherent by the time he finds Ahmed. After confronting his former
friend, George collapses and is rushed to the hospital in Jerusalem (the
very hospital where Marina wanted to take Ibrahim). He spends his
final hours in the Jewish hospital wrapped in Hebrew-marked bed-
clothes.

With no real human connections on the West Bank (her marriage to
Hassan beyond repair), Marina is torn between returning to the
United States or honoring her father's memory and her heritage by re-
maining near Jerusalem to lay claim to her ancestral land and property.

HISTORICAL BACKGROUND

The historical context for *Martyrs' Crossing* is, of course, the longtime conflict between Jew and Arabs since 1948. Following World
War II, after the discovery of the brutality attendant to the Holocaust,
when Jews throughout Europe were tortured and killed, efforts were
made by the newly established United Nations to establish an independent Jewish state. From the time the United Nations partitioned
the former Palestine state and officially created Israel in 1948, major
conflicts arose between the Palestinians (and their other Arab supporters) and the Israelis (Jews). The Arab-Israeli War of 1948–1949
ensued, with five Arab nations (Egypt, Transjordan, Syria, Lebanon,
and Iraq) immediately attacking Israel. From 1948 on, many other
conflicts would occur, with Israel increasingly occupying territory beyond its official 1948 boundaries. In what became known as the Six-
Day War of 1967, Israel expanded into the Golan Heights (formerly
of Syria), into the West Bank (formerly of Jordan), and into the Gaza
Strip (formerly of Egypt). Palestinians who had occupied the Israeli
area before 1948 fled to surrounding countries, and even more fled
the areas "occupied" by Israel in 1967. Tensions have remained constant throughout the second half of the twentieth century and now
into the twenty-first century.

George Raad provides the connection to this period in history. The
pain from those abrupt changes and from a sense of uprootedness for
the Palestinians is as palpable in the novel's late 1990s setting as it
must have been in 1948. Even today, George "is still suffering from
the shock of the Israeli takeover in that unbelievable spring of 1948.
His whole life had been cut off from him when he was only eight years
old. When the family fled to Amman, George's world had changed as
if he'd been transported to an alien planet" (Wilentz, *Martyrs' Cross-*

ing, 26). This sense of loss remains with George into his adult life. He remains angry that the house he had as a youngster, along with the friends and general way of life was suddenly stripped from him. So painful are these memories that for the past 50 plus years, whenever he has returned to the area, George has never ventured to his childhood home in Jerusalem. For him, the post-1948 (Israeli) Jerusalem despoils what he once knew.

On his final trip back to the West Bank and Israel, however, following Ibrahim's death, George bravely ventures to his old house (he still has the key to the front door, which he has kept as a reminder of his exile). Now occupying the house is another of his childhood acquaintances, Leila, a Jewish girl (now woman) he befriended in the pre-Israel days. When George sees some of the furnishings there that he remembers from his childhood, property owned by his family, he is torn between being happy to reunite with an old friend and being tormented by the evidence of his family's forced exile. The force of the loss, of the past (of history), is almost too much for George to bear. When Leila tells George that she lost a son last year in a conflict in Lebanon, he has to admit to himself that as selfish as the feeling is, he takes a bit of pleasure in knowing that Leila has had "to pay *some* price for taking away [his] land and living in [his] house for fifty years and for eternity" (244). Yet while George feels a sense of loss and sacrifice, those representing the Israelis locate for themselves a sense of achievement and cultural pride.

When Daniel Yizhar recalls the stories from his grandfather about 1948, he focuses solely on a Jewish triumph that he considers to be "morally sound" (189). Because his grandfather had fled pogroms (official persecutions or massacres) in the Ukraine before coming to what was then Palestine, Yizhar feels that his ancestors' persecutions paid for the right to establish and inhabit Israel. Yizhar thinks of his ancestors as brave men who fought only for what was just. For him, history is not so much a burden (as it is with George) but a responsibility. It is his responsibility to protect the state of Israel at all cost.

This novel is comprehensive in assessing the effect of the past on the present. All of the characters are influenced by circumstances beyond their control because decisions made decades ago along ethnic and religious lines have had a long-lasting impact. Nevertheless, *Martyrs' Crossing* instructs that inasmuch as human beings may feel unempowered and trapped by their circumstances and by the unyielding force of history, their primary goal must always be to preserve humanity. As George contemplates the meaning of life and history, he concludes: "History was history, and not as reversible as we might wish, it turned out. It was to be confronted, not denied" (237).

LITERARY ANALYSIS

Martyrs' Crossing addresses the ethnic and religious conflict between Arabs and Jews in and around Israel. It provides a very personal account of the animosity that has been sustained for over one-half century. While the novel is set primarily in the Middle East, a minor American backdrop provides a somewhat objective context for considering the conflict, the United States' longstanding support of Israel notwithstanding. In fact, that two of the major characters, George and Marina, are both Palestinian and American contributes to the more objective appraisal. The U.S. context offers up another opportunity to consider the problem of race and racial conflict, beyond the traditional conflicts prevalent on U.S. soil.

One of the prevailing themes in the novel, as would be true in any race-based debate, is individual perception versus the blind acceptance of stereotypes. Presented quite early in the novel is how Arabs and Jews, from a group perspective, consider each other. The Arabs despise the Jews for taking over their homeland back in 1948; they feel controlled by the Jewish presence in Israel, especially since Israeli authorities decide who can and cannot enter Israel. The Arabs believe the Jews have a bloated sense of superiority and that they use every opportunity to exploit Arabs. On the other hand, the Jews consider the Arabs as uncivil types who terrorize Israelis with frequent violent attacks. The Jews, now some 50 years after occupying the former Palestine, feel ownership over the land they inhabit, and they look upon Arab insurgence as a form of trespass. Each group believes the other to be completely at variance with its own sense of humanity and cultural stability. At every chance of compromise and negotiation, these old stereotypes emerge to thwart potential progress.

Functioning now in this embattled environment is Marina, who because of the loss of her child has every reason to intensify the indoctrinated hatred of the Israelis. Both she and Doron find themselves at a bizarre crossroads. Doron's individual act of compassion, albeit too late, forces this unlikely pair to reconsider their feelings about the opposing group. When Doron first meets Marina on the night she seeks entry into Israel, he is struck not only by the emergency at hand (Ibrahim's illness), but also by this mother's strength and determination to secure medical attention for her son. On this night, Marina is not simply some Palestinian woman (one of many whom Doron has seen over the years). Instead, she is a mother, an individual, whose emotional duress speaks to Doron in some profound way. Perhaps the fact that he still lives with his own mother and is in daily receipt of her love and support compels Doron to consider Marina beyond the political frame he has been commanded to enforce. At one point during their initial encounter, Doron even wishes that Marina was not the enemy.

As Marina continues to work through her grief, she is forced to realize that Doron is not to blame for Ibrahim's death; that were it not for the political burdens controlling him, Doron would have acted with compassion much sooner. So rather than lumping Doron in with all of the Israelis, Marina has to consider his individual nature and consequently acknowledge his humanity, ethnic and religious differences notwithstanding. Making this discovery is not easy for Marina; in fact, it would be easier for her to cling to the stereotypes about Israeli oppression and inhumanity. Still, Marina wrestles with her views: "She was furious with the soldier. She couldn't bear the thought of him. But there was no denying one thing. He had been trying to be on their side. She could never admit it to Hassan, because Hassan could never allow it to be true. His whole world was built on another point of view" (157). Marina is in the process of seeing this man, not as an Israeli soldier with the attendant prejudices that particular perspective brings, but as a person who himself attempted to look beyond stereotypes. For both Doron and Marina, however, viewing each other as individuals is not an easy task, as it requires the kind of intellectual fortitude that pierces through a lifetime of indoctrination or "a whole world built on another point of view."

This conflict between individual perception and group identity/ stereotyping also affects the relationship between George and Ahmed. A man still dedicated to the cause of Palestinian freedom, George wants desperately to see Ahmed as his childhood chum who is also committed to the integrity of the cause. In this way, George clings to the past. However, as Ahmed has shown him time and time again during their adult years, he is committed only to promoting his own advancement. Just as Marina must accept the individual Doron (a would-be enemy) as one who tried to be a friend, George must view Ahmed as he truly is: a self-serving Palestinian who would knowingly hurt the cause if doing so ensured self-aggrandizement. As painful as the truth may be, George must accept the fact that "the man who was

destroying the fabric of George's past was a part of that past himself."
Even though George finds it difficult to "reconcile himself to the paradox," he must admit that "he [is] beginning to feel he might hate
Ahmed now" (231). In short, this theme compels both the reader and
the characters within the novel to see good and bad in both groups
and to assess individual motivation over group politics.

Martyrs' Crossing also confronts thematically the relationship between the political and the personal. On the one hand, for the Palestinians like George, the conflict with the Israelis is a highly personal
affair. The historical removal from their homeland cuts to the core of
their being, and for those who still remember being forced out of the
former Palestine, there is an immediacy and intensity to the cause that
has never abated. For Marina, however, the "personal" aspect of this
conflict takes on a different dimension. Because she is a Boston-born
American whose link to the Middle East, prior to her arrival there four
years earlier, has been reportage from her father, Marina does not have
the kind of personal investment that George and Hassan (even more
radical than George, of course) have. Even George scoffs at Marina's
Ivy League degrees in Palestinian history and Middle East political science. For him the only true education is the personal education of having lived through the Catastrophe (Palestinian removal from the
homeland). Marina, therefore, does not feel the "personal" intensity of
this issue until the death of her child. This particular loss compels her
to question, at the dawning of the twenty-first century, the rationale
for this continued political debate. Marina wants to hate the Jews; she
wants to blame Doron. But with the loss of Ibrahim, she feels such an
emptiness that she cannot even fathom the purpose of all of this anymore. Her individual sacrifice has made dedication to the cause much
less attractive. Marina "wanted to be in a place where nothing mattered
very much and nothing was worth it, and no one had to make any final
sacrifices. She wanted to remove herself from history" (302).

This novel forces readers to question the worthiness of individual
loss in the face of political commitment, especially when the politics
are clearly burdened with corruption and half-truths. *Martyrs' Crossing*, with its emphasis on the plural *martyrs*, asks how many more individuals like Ibrahim (with his life), Marina (with her son and her
marriage), Hassan (with his son and his domestic tranquility), Doron
(with his reputation and his military position), and George (with his
intellectual and emotional energy and ultimately his life) will be sacri-
ficed in the name of so-called progress.

BIBLIOGRAPHY

Fischbach, Michael R. *Records of Dispossession: Palestinian Refugee Property and the Arab-Israeli Conflict.* New York: Columbia University Press, 2003.

Ganim, As'ad. *The Palestinian-Arab Minority in Israel, 1948–2000: A Political Study.* Albany: State University of New York Press, 2001.

Gelber, Yoav. *Palestine, 1948: War, Escape, and the Emergence of the Palestinian Refugee Problem.* Portland, OR: Sussex Academic Press, 2001.

Khalidi, Rashid. *Palestinian Identity: The Construction of Modern National Consciousness.* New York: Columbia University Press, 1997.

Kook, Rebecca B. *The Logic of Democratic Exclusion: African Americans in the United States and Palestinian Citizens in Israel.* Lanham, MD: Lexington Books, 2002.

Palestine History Web site, "History," Esam Shashaa, www.palestinehistory. com (accessed May 17, 2004).

Rouhana, Nadim N. *Palestinian Citizens in an Ethnic Jewish State: Identities in Conflict.* New Haven, CT: Yale University Press, 1997.

Wilentz, Amy. *Martyrs' Crossing.* New York: Ballantine, 2001.

Selected Bibliography

Bayor, Ronald H. *Race and Ethnicity in America: A Concise History.* New York: Columbia University Press, 2003.

Chai, Arlene. *The Last Time I Saw Mother.* New York: Fawcett, 1995.

Ciresi, Rita. *Sometimes I Dream in Italian.* New York: Random House, 2000.

Cisneros, Sandra. *The House on Mango Street.* New York: Vintage, 1991; originally published in 1984.

Corlett, J. Angelo. *Race, Racism, and Reparations.* Ithaca, NY: Cornell University Press, 2003.

Craven, Margaret. *I Heard the Owl Call My Name.* New York: Dell, 1973.

Darder, Antonia, and Rodolfo D. Torres. *After Race: Racism after Multiculturalism.* New York: New York University Press, 2004.

Essed, Philomena. *Understanding Everyday Racism: An Interdisciplinary Theory.* Newbury Park, CA: Sage, 1991.

Eze, Emmanuel Chukwudi. *Achieving Our Humanity: The Idea of the Postracial Future.* New York: Routledge, 2001.

Fishbein, Harold D. *Peer Prejudice and Discrimination: The Origins of Prejudice.* Mahwah, NJ: Erlbaum, 2002.

Goldberg, David Theo, ed. *Anatomy of Racism.* Minneapolis: University of Minnesota Press, 1990.

Holt, Thomas C. *The Problem of Race in the Twenty-First Century.* Cambridge, MA: Harvard University Press, 2000.

Keefe, Susan E., and Amado M. Padilla. *Chicano Ethnicity.* Albuquerque: University of New Mexico Press, 1987.

Keller, Nora Okja. *Fox Girl.* New York: Penguin, 2002.

Lamont, Michele. *The Cultural Territories of Race: Black and White Boundaries.* Chicago: University of Chicago Press, 1999.

Lee, Harper. *To Kill a Mockingbird.* New York: Warner, 1982; originally published in 1960.

Levine, Michael P., and Tamas Pataki, eds. *Racism in Mind.* Ithaca, NY: Cornell University Press, 2004.

Lipsitz, George. *The Possessive Investment in Whiteness: How White People Profit from Identity Politics.* Philadelphia: Temple University Press, 1998.

Potok, Chaim. *The Chosen.* New York: Ballantine, 1967.

Silko, Leslie Marmon. *Ceremony.* New York: Penguin, 1977.

Takaki, Ronald, ed. *From Different Shores: Perspectives on Race and Ethnicity in America.* New York: Oxford University Press, 1987

Twain, Mark. *The Adventures of Huckleberry Finn.* New York: Penguin, 1985; originally published in 1885.

Villarreal, Jose Antonio. *Pocho.* New York: Doubleday, 1959.

Waller, James. *Prejudice Across America.* Jackson: University Press of Mississippi, 2000.

Wilentz, Amy. *Martyrs' Crossing.* New York: Ballantine, 2001.

Wright, Richard. *Native Son.* New York: Perennial, 1998; originally published in 1940.

Yancey, George A. *Who is White? Latinos, Asians, and the New Black/Nonblack Divide.* Boulder, CO: Lynne Rienner, 2003.

Zelinsky, Wilbur. *The Enigma of Ethnicity: Another American Dilemma.* Iowa City: University of Iowa Press, 2001.

Index

About the Author

CHARLES E. WILSON, JR. is University Professor and Professor of English at Old Dominion University. His previous publications include *Walter Mosley: A Critical Companion* (2003) and *Gloria Naylor: A Critical Companion* (2001), both available from Greenwood Press.